N(V
D0403846

THE LANDSCAPE IS BEHIND THE DOOR

DATE DUE	
MAR 1 7 1995	
JUN 2 1 1996	
NOV 1 2 1997 NOV 2 8 1998	
MAR 1 1 1999	
DEC 1 0 2002	
GAYLORD	PRINTED IN U.S.A.

THE LANDSCAPE IS BEHIND THE DOOR

Pierre Martory

translated by John Ashbery

The Sheep Meadow Press
Riverdale-on-Hudson, New York

San Rafael Public Library
1100 E Street
San Rafael, CA 94901

Copyright © 1994 by Pierre Martory
Translation copyright © 1994 by John Ashbery

All rights reserved. No part of this publication may be reproduced or
transmitted in any form or by any means, electronic or mechanical,
including photocopy, recording, or any information storage and retrieval
system, without permission in writing from the publisher.

All inquiries and permission requests should be addressed to:
The Sheep Meadow Press, Post Office Box 1345,
Riverdale-on-Hudson, New York 10471.

Designed and Typeset by the Sheep Meadow Press.
Printed on acid-free paper in the United States. This book meets the
guidelines for permanence and durability of the Committee on Production
Guidelines for Book Longevity of the Council on Library Resources.

Distributed by the Sheep Meadow Press

A CIP cataloging record for this books is
available from the Library of Congress.
ISBN 1-878818-30-9

CONTENTS

INTRODUCTION

Pierre Martory's poetry is unknown in his native France. There are a number of reasons for this, the principle one being that, save for a few poems which appeared in now-forgotten little magazines in the early 1950s, Martory has never tried to publish his work or showed it to anyone (myself excepted) who might be interested in it. His only published work in France, apart from articles on music and the theater written during a 25-year stint at the weekly newsmagazine *Paris-Match*, is a novel called *Phébus ou le beau Mariage* which the firm of Denoël brought out in 1953. Despite a favorable critical reception it was not followed by another, even though Martory continues to this day to write both fiction and poetry almost constantly.

Before looking at his poetry, I have to give a few facts about his life, even though Martory shares an instinctive French antipathy for criticism mixed with biography and has asked me to keep his life out of this. But I think a little explanation in the form of a summary curriculum vitae is necessary in order for readers to approach a body of work that for me ranks with that of the finest contemporary French poets but has managed so far to escape attention even though the poet is now in his early seventies.

He was born in Bayonne in southwest France, of partly Basque ancestry. His mother died when he was two, after giving birth to a second son, Jean. His father soon remarried and had other children with his new wife. A career military officer, he was posted to Morocco, where Pierre spent much of his childhood and where he was happiest, despite life with a stepmother and an authoritarian father who never allowed his children to have any toys. Martory still visits Morocco frequently. He received his *baccalauréat* in Bayonne and in the fall of 1939 enrolled at the School of Political Sciences in Paris. In June 1940 he managed to get on the last train to leave Paris before the Germans arrived, and after a time spent at Bayonne and wandering through the south of France he traveled to Tunisia where he joined the French Army, which eventually joined forces with the invading U.S. Army.

After the war he worked at the short-lived Biarritz American

University, then as an airline clerk in Bordeaux, before moving to Paris. Here for a while he was part of a loose-knit group of writers that included Hubert Juin and Hervé Bazin, who used to meet in a café on the Ile Saint-Louis and declaim their poems to one another. This was the only time he ever frequented a literary milieu. In 1952 he went to Munich for a year, where he studied singing informally; on his return he found the group had dispersed. After the publication of his novel, which was overseen by the distinguished editor Robert Kanters, he wrote a second one which Kanters, himself a homosexual, rejected on account of its homosexual theme. (In those days, before the arrival on the scene of Barthes, Foucault and others, homosexuality was very much taboo in intellectual circles; today the climate is drastically changed.) Martory submitted a third novel to Kanters, who liked it but asked him to change the ending; in a fit of pique Martory withdrew the book and never tried to publish anything else. Years later, in his memoirs, Kanters wondered what had happened to the brilliant young author of *Phébus*, and Martory couldn't resist writing him a note reminding him that he had played a certain role in his withdrawal from the scene.

I first met Martory in 1956 while in France on a Fulbright scholarship. We soon became very close friends and remain so to this day. Pierre, a voracious and omnivorous reader with a preference for history, biography and memoirs (he reread those of Saint-Simon in their mammoth entirety after an improved Pléiade edition appeared) was the ideal guide to France and things French for an American; in addition, his take on them has something distinctly and irreverently American about it. He has always had more American friends (and Moroccan ones) than French, and says that he loves France but detests the French!

Even with Pierre's help it took me a long time to become fluent in French, and thus I began to read his poetry only after we had known each other for a year or more. I was also reading other contemporary and classical French poetry, and as I became familiar with its tropes it began to strike me that his was quite different. He had assimilated the moderns, especially René Char, as well as the classical "canon" that French students are forced to ingest, but my still relatively unschooled eye could find no resemblances, or very few, between his poetry and French poetry of the past or present. In fact, with the exception of a few older poets such as Char and Ponge, French poetry in the decade following World War II was in a period of doldrums. Something similar had happened in England, where the thirties trio of Auden, F.T. Prince and Nicholas Moore had been supplanted by Larkin's austerity; and in America, where Delmore Schwartz and the early Jarrell and Berryman were eclipsed by Lowell and the later Auden, Berryman and Jarrell.

Looking today for antecedents to Martory's poetry I am forced to speculate, since for some reason we rarely discuss our work with each other. His fluency in German makes me aware of trace-elements of Hölderlin, Rilke and Trakl (the latter especially in "Red and Black Lake"), though again these are only educated guesses. We both share an enthusiasm for Raymond Roussel, whose otherworldly landscapes are perhaps "behind the door," especially in a longish poem called "Evenings in Rochefort" which I translated for the review *Locus Solus* in the sixties, but which Martory preferred not to reprint in this collection. In the end the only fruitful comparison seems to be with Rimbaud, and not because Martory's poetry resembles his, but because both are similar in resembling no one else. It is difficult for French poets to escape the crystalline tyranny of the French language; even the Surrealists at their most fantastic built on classical foundations. Only in recent years, as younger French poets have become aware of new American experiments with language, and vice versa (thanks in some degree to the cross-pollinating efforts of *Américainistes* like Emmanuel Hocquard and Serge Fauchereau), has our younger generation begun to have an impact in France; meanwhile, a spate of recent translations has enabled English-speaking readers to assess the achievements of major figures such as Edmond Jabès and Michel Deguy, and of such innovative younger poets as Pascalle Monnier and Anne Portugal.

Whether Martory has been influenced by American models I don't know, though when we first met he was reading Emily Dickinson, Eliot and Gertrude Stein. He certainly hadn't read my poetry yet, though I find a curious prefiguring of it in poems of his written before we met, such as "Blues" and "Ma Chandelle est morte." And after I began translating him, that is, after I began to realize that his marvelous poetry would likely remain unknown unless I translated it and brought it to the attention of American readers (fortunately this Sheep Meadow edition will be distributed in France in a French edition) I have begun to find echoes of his work in mine. His dreams, his pessimistic résumés of childhood that are suddenly lanced by a joke, his surreal loves, his strangely lit landscapes with their inquisitive birds and disquieting flora, are fertile influences for me, though I hope I haven't stolen anything—well, better to steal than borrow, as Eliot more or less said. I can only hope that this first substantial gathering of Martory's poetry into a volume will be a revelation for others as well.

John Ashbery

à J.A. avec affection et admiration

THE LANDSCAPE IS BEHIND THE DOOR

MA CHANDELLE EST MORTE

La chambre de ma mère a du papier à fleurs
Du papier à fleurs de papier
Ma mère avortera d'un prince rouge et noir
D'un gnome à la lèvre fendue
Mille raies bleues et jaunes enchantent mes réveils
Je reste le plus beau le plus sage
Je reste le meilleur des fils de ma mère
Et ma mère au profil dessiné sur le mur
Est sortie tôt pour boire des absinthes
Ou acheter du pain ou laver ma culotte
Ou vendre ma culotte et la sienne à personne
Souris au fromage rouge le temps passe
Souris ma soeur grise tu parles avec tes ongles
Un trou cache un piège
Un soir cache un jour
Un matin n'est jamais qu'une nuit fatiguée
De ce jour trop pareil au jour par la fenêtre.

MA CHANDELLE EST MORTE

My mother's bedroom has flowered wallpaper
Wallpaper with paper flowers
My mother will abort a black and red prince
A gnome with a harelip
A thousand blue and yellow stripes delight my wakings
I remain the handsomest the wisest
I remain the best of my mother's sons
And my mother with her profile drawn on the wall
Has gone out early to drink absinthe
Or buy bread or wash my underpants
Or sell my underpants and hers to no one
Mouse with red cheese time is passing
Mouse my gray sister you speak with your nails
A hole hides a trap
An evening hides a day
A morning is never anything but a tired evening
Of this day too much like the day beyond the window.

CE QUE JE DIS, PEUT-ETRE, N'EST PAS VRAI

Les cinémas sont pleins d'ombres:
Un passé qui sera l'avenir permanent.
On entend parler des langues très anciennes
Des bouches un trait au crayon
Rouge restauré mille fois.
Et la chair vive et le coeur maltraité
La main qui cherche une main
Eprouvent de délicieux soulèvements
Immarcessibles
Un plaisir pareil à celui
Que donne la soif apaisée
Un soir
D'été trop lourd de joies.

Parmi les odeurs recrées
Un parfum venu de quelque
Lointain atavisme
Fait surgir sous la lumière démodée
Un décor comme un rêve
Décousu de tout réel
Dans lequel une fille un garçon
Si l'on en juge par leur voix
Se roulent sur une écharpe abandonnée
Cherchent la trace la sueur
Le passage d'un autre
Son amant son frère sa soeur
Lui-même
Sa raison d'être
Sa mort.

Les jours de pluie, plus
Un bateau sur l'horizon. La mer
Sera un Sahara.
Et seul parmi les survivants déçus
Un enfant remplira de mémoire

WHAT I SAY, PERHAPS, ISN'T TRUE

The cinemas are full of shadows:
A past that will be the permanent future.
One hears very ancient languages spoken
From mouths a red pencil line
Redrawn a thousand times.
And the living flesh and the abused heart
The hand that seeks a hand
Experience delightful
Incorruptible upheavals
A pleasure equal to the one that
Quenched thirst gives
On a summer evening
Too heavy with pleasures.

Among the recreated odors
A perfume arrived from some
Distant atavism
Causes scenery like a dream
To rise up in the old-fashioned lighting
Unstitched from anything real
In which a girl a boy
To judge from their voices
Are rolling on an abandoned scarf
Searching for the trace the sweat
The passing of someone else
His lover his brother his sister
Himself
His reason for being
His death.

The days of rain then
A boat on the horizon. The sea
Will be a Sahara
And alone among the disappointed survivors
A child will fill the pages

Les pages,
Son œuvre millefeuille,
Le long déroulement de son
Calvaire (c'est trop dire).
Mais là, sans témoin ni
Complice, il fondra dans l'immensité
De l'instant,
Jusqu'à n'être plus qu'une
Goutte de cette pluie
Dans toute mer.

With memory
His thousand-page opus,
The long unfolding of his
Calvary (that's too strong a word).
But there, with neither witness nor
Accomplice, he'll melt in the immensity
Of the instant,
Till he becomes just another
Drop of that rain
In that sea.

SUR LE PONT-MARIE

A qui le dire? Je crache des ronds
Je crache dans l'eau de la rivière
La nuit. Les épouvantes se rassemblent
Sans figure sans voix comme
Une absence qui ne commençe pas.

La peur m'agrippe au parapet.
Pierre qui moud le grain de mon nom
Qui prolonge sa rigoureuse sensation
Le long des allers et retours
Sur le pont de chaque à chaque rive,
Refusant un chemin pour rentrer quelque part.

Savoir où je veux entrer sinon
Dans l'eau de cette rivière cette nuit
Par un crachat d'abord, puis une main
Qui lâche la pierre et bat le vide
Et griffe l'arche ouverte de la pierre dans l'eau,
Par mes cheveux affranchis de pesanteur
Dans ce saut, et mes yeux déchirant les couleurs renversées
Les signaux verts et rouges, flammes
Sous les cieux reflétés par les eaux.

Non je ne puis imaginer ma bouche suffocant
Mes poumons remplis d'eau
Ni la dernière image accrochée à mes yeux
L'instant où je la perds en cet instant
D'éternité finie à peine commencée.

A qui le dire? Je crache des ronds,
Je crache dans l'eau de la rivière la nuit.
Les épouvantes se rassemblent sans voix comme
Une absence qui ne finira pas.

ON THE PONT-MARIE

Who can I tell it to? I'm spitting rings
I'm spitting in the river water at night.
The terrors are gathering
Faceless voiceless like an absence
That doesn't begin.

Fear clamps me to the parapet.
Stone that mills the grain of my name pierre
Prolonging its rigorous feeling
Along the comings and goings on the bridge
Of each to each bank,
Refusing a path that would lead somewhere like home.

To know where I want to go if not
Into the water of this river this night
First with a blob of spit, then a hand
That lets go of the stone and flails the empty air
And claws the empty arch between stone and water,
With my hair freed from gravity
Then with this leap and my eyes tearing the overturned colors
Green and red signals, flames
Under the sky reflected in the water.

No I can't imagine my mouth suffocating
My lungs swollen with water
Nor the last image fastened to my eyes
The instant I lose it in that instant
Of eternity ended when it's barely begun.

Who can I tell it to? I'm spitting rings,
I'm spitting in the river water at night.
The terrors are gathering voiceless like
An absence that won't end.

DIMANCHE ET FETES

Que l'on dédie ce jour au bonheur! J'ai monté
Des chevaux sur les airs d'un lointain opéra.
Ce manège et le ciel tournent comme la voix
Des enfants qui rient d'y être ensemble debout.

Abandonnons la ville à sa raideur de pierre
Ses bulbes ses plafonds ses rivières à ponts
Escaladons les toits jusqu'aux paratonnerres
Jusqu'au soleil tout nu que l'on touche du doigt.

Prenons congé des croix et des alléluias
Etouffons de baisers les sirènes guerrières
Offrons-nous pour fêter ce dimanche un bouquet de
Mille fleurs comme chants de cloches à midi.

SUNDAYS AND HOLIDAYS

May this day be dedicated to happiness! I have ridden
Horses to the tunes of a distant opera.
This carousel and the sky turn like the voice
Of children laughing to be there standing together.

Let's leave the city to its stony stiffness
Its bulbs its ceilings its rivers with bridges
Let's climb the roofs as far as the lightning-rods
As far as the naked sun you can touch with your finger.

Let's say farewell to crosses and alleluias
Let's smother the warrior sirens with kisses
To celebrate this Sunday let's buy ourselves a bouquet
Of a thousand flowers like songs of the bells at noon.

EN BAS DES MARCHES

C'était moi l'enfant dans la poussette
Qui descendait l'escalier d'Odessa.
Je criais, mais vous ne pouviez pas m'entendre
Puisque le film était muet.
Je hurlais: "A mort Bakounine! A mort
Le tsar et la flotte rouge! A mort
Celui qui inventa cette voiture pour bébés
Alors qu'il est si doux d'être porté
Endormi, de mourir peut-être
Sur le sein d'une femme aux joues roses et aux
    tresses jaunes!..."

Au pied des marches ils ramassèrent
Ma cervelle avec une cuillère d'argent.

Depuis ce jour je descends comme un fou
Toutes les marches d'escalier de vos vies,
Et je continue a crier: "A bas
Jéhovah, Jésus, Mahomet et autres fétiches
Qui prétendent ouvrir les portes d'éternité!
A bas les grands hommes gavés d'arrogance
Qui instillent le fanatisme dans les coeurs!
A mort César, à bas la conquête du monde
A mort les révolutions l'argent le pouvoir!
Je veux un monde sans escaliers
Je veux dormir sur les rives de la Mer Noire
Dans les bras d'une grosse grasse babouchka rose
Qui chante pour moi seul une berceuse."

AT THE BOTTOM OF THE STEPS

I was the child in the baby carriage
Rolling down the Odessa steps.
I cried, but you couldn't hear me
Because the film was silent.
I yelled: "Death to Bakunin! Death
To the czar and the red fleet! Death
To the inventor of this baby carriage
When it's so sweet to be carried,
Asleep, maybe dying,
On the bosom of a woman with pink cheeks and
    yellow braids!..."

At the bottom of the steps they scooped up
My brains with a silver spoon.

Since that day I roll like a lunatic
Down all the steps of the stairway of your lives,
And I go on screaming: "Down with
Jehovah, Jesus, Mohammed and other fetishes
Who claim to unlock the gates of eternity!
Down with the great men stuffed with arrogance
Who poison our hearts with fanaticism!
Death to Caesar, down with the conquest of the world,
Death to revolutions, money, power!
I want a world without stairs
I want to sleep on the shores of the Black Sea
In the arms of a fat pink babushka
Who'll sing a lullaby only to me."

LE PAYSAGE EST DERRIERE LA PORTE

Le paysage est derrière la porte.
Le personnage est là… New York est plein
D'endroits pareils où se construit
Un monde, une nuée. Seules
Les têtes restent en place. On paye
Avant d'arriver, longtemps avant
D'ouvrir la bouche. Il y a près de nous
Des choses qui ont tous leurs côtés verts.

Les yeux se portent et se perdent.
Une chenille fait la différence.
La fille au sang plein le visage
S'arrête et demande l'heure.
C'est une année qui ne sait pas son nombre:
Un sourire au fond d'une poche.
Tiens! l'oiseau menteur frère des confidences
Quitte le lit familier des ruisseaux:
La vie des autres peinte sur la lampe.

"Je te touche comme une paye.
Tu es ma statue superflue
Couvée sous de chaudes larmes.
Je creuse jusqu' aux antipodes
Je déroule les bandelettes, l'horoscope:
C'est mon corps, c'est mon cocon, surpris
Dans un sommeil de sable prolifique
Que je découvre, cyclope évanoui."

Il suffirait d'entrer, de s'asseoir
Près d'un livre, de plier l'ombre
A ses genoux, de savoir qui
Marche sur le lit, passe le miroir.
La poussière grise le linge
Les photos étouffent de nuit.
Or rien n'apparait dans la chambre
Sinon le paysage inaccessible dehors.

Là-bas, les feux de la préhistoire s'obstinent
A luire. La felouque égarée porte un squelette

THE LANDSCAPE IS BEHIND THE DOOR

The landscape is behind the door.
The person is there... New York is full
Of similar places where a world,
A large cloud, is being built. Only
The heads stay put. You pay
Before arriving, a long time before
Opening your mouth. There are things
Near us which all have their green sides.

You wear your eyes and lose them.
A caterpillar makes the difference.
The girl whose face is full of blood
Stops and asks the time.
It's a year that doesn't know its number:
A smile at the bottom of a pocket.
Look! the liar-bird, brother of secrets,
Leaves the familiar creek bed:
The life of others painted on a lampshade.

"I draw you like a salary.
You are my superfluous statue
Hatched beneath hot tears.
I'm digging toward the antipodes.
I unwind the bandages, the horoscope:
It's my body, it's my cocoon, surprised
In a sleep of prolific sand,
That I'm uncovering, like a Cyclops that fainted."

It would be enough to enter, to sit
Near a book, to fold the shadow
To one's knees, to know who
Walks on the bed, who passes the mirror.
Dust tints the linens gray.
Photos choke on night.
Now nothing is visible in the room
Except the inaccessible landscape outdoors.

Down there, the fires of prehistory continue stubbornly
To glow. The lost felucca ferries a skeleton

A son tombeau. Un disque alimente le ciel.
Aux creux des geysers les dauphins
Profitent de l'incognito pour pleurer.
Une main religieuse étrangle la pitié
Et glisse dans la boîte aux lettres
La tristesse parfumée du silence.

La porte placardée de tels instants
Ne s'ouvre pas. Les cigarettes en fumée
Déroulées comme l'accessoire beauté
Laissent aux doigts l'odeur du temps passé.
L'intelligence géomètre arpente
La distance de dedans à dehors.
Tout est en place, rien ne manque.
De guerre lasse l'abeille contre
La vitre finit par renoncer à la fleur.

To its grave. A disc feeds the sky.
In the hollows of geysers dolphins are taking
Advantage of their incognito to cry.
A pious hand is strangling the pity
And slips into the letter-box
The perfumed sadness of silence.

The door placarded with such moments
Doesn't open. The cigarettes unrolled
In smoke (a supplementary beauty)
Leave on the fingers the smell of time past.
Intelligence like a geometer paces
The distance from inside to outside.
Everything is in place, nothing is missing.
Weary of strife the bee on
The windowpane finally renounces the flower.

SOUS L'ORME

Sous l'orme depuis très longtemps
Je t'attends, ô mon âme.
Les semaines se suivent comme des livres
Qu'on parcourt la tête ailleurs
Pleine de musique elle aussi distraite
D'un profond bourdonnement où les mots les images
Les perceptions reposent dans le magma de mémoire
Dont est fait notre esprit.
Et rien ne vient affirmer ta venue,
Nul indice autre que fumée.
Est-ce toi qu'il aurait fallu accueillir
Quand la tendresse gonflait le coeur?
Toi qu'il fallait découvrir
Sur les rivages de la pitié ou de l'amour?
On ne m'a pas appris à reconnaitre ta présence
Même quand les réveils soulèvent les membres
D'un bonheur à venir; même quand
Fatigué d'un long jour je cherche
Dans l'immense silence obscur où je bascule
Ce qui différencie le soleil de la mort.
Heures accumulées, richesse dérisoire,
Je suis prêt à quitter les arbres et les villes
Mais j'espère toujours te recevoir, mon âme,
Chargée de ma propre éternité.
Toi qui es moi, qui ne ressembles à personne,
Toi que je dois rendre un jour à qui sait qui.

UNDER THE ELM

Under the elm for a long time
I've been waiting for you, O my soul.
Weeks follow each other like books
Perused, my thoughts elsewhere,
Full of music that's distracted too
Full of a deep buzzing where words images
Perceptions dwell in the jumble of memory
Of which our mind is composed.
And nothing comes to assert your coming
No other sign than smoke.
Is it you that we should have welcomed
When tenderness filled our hearts?
You that we should have discovered
On the shores of pity or of love?
I have not been taught to notice your presence
Even when reveille raises the limbs
Of a future happiness; even when
Tired of a long day I seek
Silence in the immense dark where I jettison
What differentiates the sun from death.
Hours accumulated, absurd riches,
I am ready to give up the trees and the cities
But I still hope to receive you, my soul,
Laden with my own eternity.
You who are me, who resembles nobody,
You that I must give back some day to who knows who.

DUNE

"Les cygnes amputés de leurs ailes violettes"
Disais-tu, en jetant les pages aux roseaux
D'un livre : Mrs Dalloway.
L'herbe nue battait un cadre de papier doré
La moisissure. C'était une vignette à peine vierge
Sous la pluie. Et soudain
Ni toi ni moi n'étions plus là ou pas encore.
Nous avions disparu derrière la plus haute dune d'Europe
Elle-même se déplaçant dans l'espace et le temps
Grain de sable après grain de sable.

Je me suis roulé sur tes mains,
J'ai léché tes genoux, ton ventre. La bouche
Pleine de galets j'ai cessé de bégayer
Mon nom. Il me semblait que le sable
Tremblait derrière moi sous des pas.
Je me retournais. Derrière moi
Personne, sinon toi qui criais "Es-tu là?"

J'étais là.

L'arbre au lointain pencha un peu sous le vent.
La fumée des vapeurs, le parfum des pins écrasés…
Un nid creusé sous mon aisselle:
L'oiseau y dépose ses oeufs.
Je les couve, tenus par des sangles cruelles
Et mon sang gicle sous ma peau.
C'est là la blessure que je me suis faite
En cherchant la blessure que tu m'as faite.

Les pavillons glissent devant la fenêtre
Le soleil tombe dans la coupe de jaspe.
Un très lent crissement de métal mouillé…

Demain il fera beau dit la radio.

DUNE

"The swans with their purple wings amputated"
You said, throwing to the reeds pages
Of a book: Mrs. Dalloway.
The naked grass was beating a gilt frame on a page:
Mildew. It was a barely virgin text illustration
In the rain. And suddenly
Neither I nor you were there or not yet.
We had disappeared behind the highest dune in Europe
The dune itself moving into space and time
Grain after grain of sand.

I have rolled around on your hands,
I have licked your knees, your belly. My mouth
Full of pebbles I have stopped stuttering
My name. It seemed to me that the sand
Was trembling behind me under footfalls.
I turned round. Behind me
No one, unless you who screamed "Are you there?"

I was there.

The distant tree bent a little in the wind.
The steamers' smoke, the perfume of trodden pine needles…
A nest hollowed under my armpit:
The bird leaves its eggs there.
I hatch them, fastened by cruel bands
And my blood spurts under my skin.
There is the wound I gave myself
While I was looking for the wound you gave me.

The ship's pennants are gliding past the window
The sun is sinking in the jasper cup.
A very slow squeaking of wet metal…

Tomorrow the weather will be fair says the radio.

UN DIMANCHE A MONFORT-L'AMAURY

Un oeuf vert couvé sous la neige
Un oeuf couvert d'idéogrammes

Si le petit train stoppe aux marges des cartes
N'en profite pas pour filer par le trou de la baignoire

L'artiste rétablit sur le gazon
Son équilibre perdu aux grilles du balcon

Nous avions vu ensemble les pires paysages
Regrettant le noir et blanc du cinématographe

Quand nous rentrions plus loin du chien que près du loup
Personne pour nous accueillir à grands coups de courroux

A Cadix pour mieux écouter les castagnettes
Nous avions meurtri nos mains à quelques espagnolettes

La lune ravageant d'exquises mosaiques
Gardait le moelleux de flûtes maghrébines

Aujourd'hui tinte encore à l'abri des curieux
L'argentin boléro d'un cymbalon quinteux

Le retour s'effectua par une nuit incommensurable
Peuplée de chats enroués d'anglaises lasses

Un rideau dont la soie brûle
Ne cache plus qu'un souvenir ridicule

Un oeuf vert couvé sous la neige
Un oeuf couvert d' idéogrammes.

A SUNDAY IN MONFORT-L'AMAURY

A green egg incubating under the snow
An egg covered with ideograms

If the little train stops at the maps' margins
Don't seize the occasion to escape down the bathtub drain

The acrobat re-establishes on the lawn
The balance he lost on the balcony railing

Together we had seen the worst landscapes
Regretting the cinematographer's black and white

When we came back, far from the dog, close to the wolf's path,*
There was no one to welcome us with great bursts of wrath

At Cádiz, the better to hear the castanets,
We bruised our hands grappling with some espagnolettes

The moon, laying waste to exquisite mosaics
Still kept the mellowness of Maugrabin flutes

Today, shielded from inquisitive comers,
The Argentine bolero still tinkles on catarrhal dulcimers

The return was accomplished on an incommensurable night
Peopled with hoarse-voiced cats and weary Englishwomen

A curtain whose silk is ablaze
Conceals nothing more than a stupid lost phrase

A green egg incubating under the snow
An egg covered with ideograms

*"*entre chien et loup*" (halfway between dog and wolf) is a common French
　　expression for twilight, a time when it would be difficult to distinguish
　　between a wolf and a dog seen from a distance. (Tr.)

LA CAGE

Etes-vous entré dans la cage? La plus vide?
Soudain tout glisse de l'autre côté sans à-coup:
Les arbres, les maisons, les promeneurs, les journaux;
Soudain tout est balayé de ses couleurs accoutumées,
Le sens des vents, le déroulement des après-midi;
Soudain tout est oublié: la géométrie, la poésie,
Le poids du coeur, les racines, les années.
Seule s'installe une splendide faim de forêt vierge
Et c'est elle qui vous pousse à sortir de la cage.

Vous n'êtes plus le même désormais,
Pas même dans votre lit, dans les bras d'une femme,
Pas même dans vos rêves où vous arpentez un désert
Tout parcouru du fumet des gazelles;
Pas même dans la contemplation en vous de ce phénomène étrange
Dont vous perdez conscience et qui ne signifie rien pour vous.

Tout est oublié, la cage et le baillement immense de la foule,
Et la satisfaction incalculable d'être là où il faut.

THE CAGE

Have you gone into the cage? The emptiest one?
Suddenly everything slides to the other side without jarring:
Trees, buildings, pedestrians, newspapers;
Suddenly everything is swept clean of its habitual colors
The direction of the winds, the unrolling of afternoons;
Suddenly everything is forgotten: geometry, poetry,
The weight of the heart, the roots, the years.
Only a splendid virgin-forest hunger moves in
And it's that that makes you leave the cage.

Henceforth you're no longer the same,
Not even in your bed, in a woman's arms,
Not even in your dreams where you stride across a desert
Traversed by the scent of gazelles;
Not even in the contemplation in you of this strange phenomenon
Of which you lose consciousness and which means nothing to you.

Everything is forgotten, the cage and the immense yawn of the crowd,
And the incalculable satisfaction of being there where you belong.

PROSE DE BUTTES-CHAUMONT

L'auteur des ces jardins se jeta, prétends-tu,
Du haut du Temple de l' Amour, copie
Du Douglas Stewart Monument, Carlton Hill, Edimbourg,
Sauf que sur le socle ici, au centre de la colonnade,
Le petit dieu, invisible d'ailleurs sur la vue
Stéréoscopique de référence, est absent,
Prêt à être remplacé sans doute le temps d'un déclic
Par un enfant venu contempler un dimanche,
Comme nous, le panorama crevé de brumes,
La ville peinte sur un frémissement du temps.

Mais la question n'est pas là.

Je voulais te saisir la main
Et d'un coup de talon prendre essor avec toi
Comme les figures de Puvis de Chavannes
Dans Le Bois Sacré Cher Aux Muses et Aux Arts
Ou comme dans ces rêves dont nous parlions,
Où, marchant dans la foule, il suffit d'un pas plus long
Pour nous hisser au ras des têtes en évitant les becs de gaz
Les isolateurs de verre, les poteaux, les girouettes.

Comment reçoit-il ma ville, ton regard
Encore accroché à la frange hispanique de Riverside Park
Ou du côté du Flatiron?
Et moi, le sac lourd de science livresque —
Flasque butin volé aux poubelles de l' Histoire —
Qu'est-ce-que je vois qui n'est pas dans tes yeux?

Des portes à guichet
Des enseignes bleuies
Un ange bardé de cuir
Avec sa chaine en argent
Porté par des nuées
De Gitanes papier maïs
Qui examine s'il y a
Des rides autour de nos yeux
Avant de nous percer
Le ventre d'un laser...?

PROSE DES BUTTES-CHAUMONT

The creator of these gardens threw himself, so you claim,
From the top of the Temple of Cupid, a copy
Of the Douglas Stuart monument, Carlton Hill, Edinburgh,
Except that here, on the pedestal at the center of the colonnade,
The diminutive god, invisible in fact on the stereopticon
View I am consulting, is missing,
Ready to be replaced no doubt in the instant of a shutter's click
By a child who like us has come, one Sunday,
To gaze on the fog-pierced panorama,
The city painted on a tremor of time.

But that's not the question.

I wanted to seize your hand and touch bottom
So we could take off into space together
Like the figures in Puvis de Chavannes'
The Sacred Wood Beloved of the Muses and the Arts
Or like those dreams we were talking about,
Where, walking in a crowd, we have only to take a giant step
To fly away, grazing heads as we avoid the street lamps,
The glass insulators on telegraph poles, the weather vanes.

How does it take in my city, your look
Still hanging on the hispanic fringe of Riverside Park,
Or down by the Flatiron?
And I, with my sackful of bookish knowledge —
Flaccid booty stolen from the trash cans of History —
What do I see that's not in your eyes?

Gates with turnstiles
Bluish neon
A leather angel
With his silver chain
Borne on clouds
Of maize-paper Gitanes
Looking to see whether there are
Wrinkles around our eyes
Before stabbing our
Stomach with a laser...?

Une rue parcourue par d'étranges messages
Que s'envoyent les voyoux à travers la cervelle
En carton-bouilli perméable d'un flic…?

Un flot d'alcool berçant
De ses graves volutes
Des baisers que nous finirons par échanger…?

Un livre commencé manuscrit par un moine
Et achevé sur l'écran d'un ordinateur
Dans une langue talée comme figues trop mûres
Où croupit une odeur d'alphabet mal connu…?

Une femme fanée fumant dans les décombres
Sans hâte sachant bien que tout désir est mort
Serre-t-elle en sa main une graine germée
Espoir d'un arbre de la Science du Bien et du Mal…?

La rue en bas peut conduire au quai
Le quai aboutit toujours à une chambre
La chambre est toujours occupée par un lit
Le lit n'a de place que pour ton corps
Ton corps se réduit à ta bouche
Toutes les mains se posent sur des cuisses.
Enveloppons-nous de brouillards mauves.
C'est la nuit des parfums et je découvre
En m'approchant de ton bas-ventre
La place exacte où vont foisonner les cloportes.

Je te donne Paris ses paires d'yeux ses coeurs
Chacun gros comme un poing de boxeur.
Ecoute: ils accordent leur battement
Dans le ronron du silence.
Je te donne, ajoutant parole sur parole,
Les milliards de mots prononcés à cet instant.
Regarde: un seul cristal liquide c'est ton nom.
Je te donne la fournaise des corps jetés
Dans la gueule du temps. Touche:
La peau humaine électrise tes doigts.

A street traversed by odd messages
From punk to punk across the porous
Porridge of a cop's brain...?

A wave of alcohol cradling
In its solemn scrolls
Kisses we will one day exchange...?

A book begun in manuscript by a monk
And finished on the screen of a computer terminal
In a bruised language like overripe figs
Where the perfume of a little-known alphabet stagnates...?

A faded woman who's smoking amid the rubble,
Not in haste, knowing well that all desire is dead;
Does she clasp a sprouted seed,
The hope of a tree of Knowledge of Good and Evil...?

The street below probably leads to the embankment
The embankment always ends at the bedroom
The bedroom is always filled up by the bed
The bed has room only for your body
Your body is reduced to your mouth
All hands are placed on thighs.
Let's wrap ourselves in lavender fog.
It's the night of perfumes and I discover
As I approach your groin
The exact spot where wood lice will swarm.

I give you Paris its pairs of eyes its hearts
Each as big as a boxer's fist.
Listen: they're synchronizing their heartbeats
In the hum of silence.
I give you — adding speech to speech —
The billions of words pronounced at this instant.
Look: a single liquid crystal and it's your name.
I give you the furnace of bodies thrown
Into the jaws of time. Touch:
Human skin electrifies your fingers.

Tout est à toi.
Remets en sortant ton ticket de vestiaire
Personne ne criera au voleur.
La porte refermée, le ciel toujours de soufre
Roulera par tes nuits et tes nuits
Ajoutant aux images mortes des images.

De quoi est fait ce paysage des hommes
Auquel tu appartiens?
Tu t'y promènes avec moi
Sans en éprouver un vertige.
Tu es trop sûr que les abîmes
Où se perdent en bas les autres
Pour nous l'ouvriront pas.

Everything is yours
Return your coat check as you leave
No one will cry thief.
Once the door is shut the sky, still sulfur,
Will roll through your nights and your nights
Adding images to dead images.

What is it made of, this landscape of men
To which you belong?
You walk there with me,
Feeling no vertigo.
You're too sure that the abysses
In which the others are lost down there
Will not open for us.

ARCHIVES INDECHIFFRABLES

Dans cette maison où personne n'habite
Les portes s'ouvrent sur des horizons cadenassés
Les arbres peints en noir résonnent du silence
D'oiseaux desséchés attendant la résurrection
Pour peu qu'un vent suffisant souffle sur leur plumage
Révélant leur couleur leur espèce et leur sexe.

L'air pourtant imprégné d'imprécises présences
Conserve le parfum de vies anciennes oubliées
Dans des tiroirs aux serrures que gardent
(Lèvres serrées roses confites dans la glace)
Des secrets attendant d'improbables baisers
Pour mordre à mort celui qui voudrait les violer

Et demander: où sont parties les âmes immortelles?
Celle qui regardait le soir se balancer les bateaux
Celle qui brûlait sa chair pour un inaccessible amour.

Il y a quelque part dans une grotte dans un désert
Une brique d'argile marquée au coin d'un alphabet
Qui nous dirait comment le silence pesait
Au musicien privé de son orgue
Et si les larmes de l'amant délaissé
Avaient les couleurs de nos prières
Et si un coeur battait de la même angoisse haletante
Que le nôtre le soir quand sonne une cloche au lointain.

UNDECIPHERABLE ARCHIVES

In that house where no one lives
The doors open on padlocked horizons
The black-painted trees echo with the silence
Of dried birds awaiting resurrection
If enough wind ever blows on their plumage
Revealing their color their species their sex.

The air nevertheless permeated with imprecise presences
Keeps the perfume of forgotten former lives
In drawers with locks that hold
(Clenched lips roses candied in ice)
Secrets awaiting unlikely kisses
So as to bite to death the one who would violate them

And ask: where have the immortal souls gone?
The one that looked at the boats swaying at evening
The one that burned its flesh for an inaccessible lover.

There is somewhere in a cave in a desert
A clay brick stamped with an alphabet
That would tell us how the silence weighed
On the musician deprived of his clavier
And if the tears of the abandoned lover
Were the color of our prayers
And if a heart was beating with the same breathless anguish
As ours when a distant bell sounds in the evening.

URBS

De mes semelles mille pluies j'étale sur le macadam,
Bouillie de sang d'épinards d'oeufs malades,
L'alphabet mouvant du néon.
Couchée près de ce bois qu'elle prend pour son dieu,
Fille folle sincèrement d'être éternelle,
La ville s'offre en ses reflets d'hiver toujours
Chapelet de martyrs au cou, l'oeil de fumées.

Souviens-toi de Rome de Rome de Rome.
Colonnes sans feuillages autres que les flèches
Pour Sébastien déshabillé par quelque guide;
Voûtes rompues où le ciel bat des étincelles;
La cigarette à la bouche rouge, un abbé
Regrette de paiens baisers sans contrition,
Cris béats, pages roses d'un Larousse en toutes langues.

Si proches parentes cités successives
Qui ne se disent rien mais se ressemblent.
Corps corrompu où boivent leur vraie vie
Les mouches á l'échelle des fresques éteintes.
Brocart mité des vierges en majesté.
Sages saintes au regard de plâtre.
Tant d'os dorment ici dans un magasin de piété.

Souviens toi de Rome de Rome de Rome.
La nuit contre les manches en croix d'un vieil ange,
Contre un Antinoüs et son sexe élimé,
Contre Adrien pleurant derrière une chapelle,
Contre les voix hurlant à la mort d'un géant,
Les mille yeux crevés, les fausses ombres, les secrets,
Un cirque pour toujours péripathétique et sonore.

Souviens-toi de ces trous, des coupoles qui les comblent,
Des crânes embaumés, des bijoux qui les ornent,
Des oliviers jaunis sous le coca-cola,
De tes pas dans les pas d'actuels somnambules
Pressés de retrouver au détour d'un palais
Une borne où laisser leurs gants et leur sourire
Pour nager nus dans la Cloaca Maxima.

URBS

With my soles I stir up a thousand rains on the asphalt
Gruel of blood of spinach of sick eggs
The blinking alphabet of neon.
Lying near that wood she mistakes for a god
Girl sincerely mad to be eternal,
The city offers itself in its winter reflections always
Chaplet of martyrs at its throat, eye of smoke.

Remember Rome Rome Rome.
Columns with no other foliage but arrows
For Sebastian undressed by some guide;
Broken vaults where the sky beats sparks;
Cigarette at his red mouth, a priest
Longs for pagan kisses without contrition,
Blissful cries, pink pages of a Larousse in all languages.

Such near relations successive cities
Which don't speak to each other but resemble each other.
Putrid body where flies on the same scale as extinct frescoes
Drink their real life.
Moth-eaten brocade of the virgins in splendor.
Wise saints with plaster gazes.
So many bones asleep here in a shop of religious images.

Remember Rome Rome Rome.
Night against the crossed sleeves of an old angel
Against an Antinous with worn genitals
Against Hadrian weeping behind a chapel
Against voices howling at the death of a giant
The thousand eyes put out, the false shadows, the secrets,
An echoing arena where tourists stroll forever.

Remember those holes the cupolas that fill them,
The embalmed skulls, the jewels that decorate them,
The yellowing olive trees under the Coca Cola,
Your footsteps in the steps of today's sleepwalkers
Anxious to find in the angle of a palace
A milestone on which they can leave their gloves and their smile
And swim naked in the Cloaca Maxima.

DANS LE VENTRE DE LA BALEINE

Air respiré sans le savoir,
Agréable balancement doublé
D'une musique, un rêve, qui sait?
Et l'impression d'être en dehors
Du temps à attendre
Sans fin l'accomplissement
Des choses.
Sommeil éternel, durant juste
Un oisif matin, sans
Références aux visions à venir,
Aux nuits perdues.

A travers les liquides distances
S'entendent pourtant
Comme rugissements étouffés
La rumeur d'hommes traînant sur les plages
Garçons dont l'errance empoisonne les soirs.
Ils n'entendent plus la langue qu'ils parlent
Ils pleurent comme des chiens
En regardant tomber la lune
Dans cet horizon où je baigne.
Ils dévorent leur propre chair
Et font l'amour puis lacèrent leur sexe
Les yeux fermés car ils n'avaient plus de désirs.
Ils dansent parmi l'univers bousculé
Le frénétique pas des espoirs scalpés...

Sont-ils donc, ceux-là, mes semblables?
Et Seigneur suis-je sur les mêmes vagues
A me vautrer comme une truie gravide
Sur les tripes pestilentielles,
Secouée par les borborygmes
Que je croyais cordes suaves
Au flanc d'un coeur hypertrophié
Qui bat un tam-tam angélique? Suis-je
A glisser jusqu'à la matrice
Ecrin clos où le temps attend
Sans fin l'accomplissement
Des choses?

IN THE BELLY OF THE WHALE

Air breathed in without my knowing it,
Pleasant swaying that rhymes
With a certain music, a dream, who knows?
And the impression of being outside
Of time to await
Endlessly the completion
Of things.
Eternal sleep lasting only
An idle morning without
Reference to the visions to come,
To the lost nights.

Through the liquid expanses
However one can still hear
Something like a stifled roar
The noise of men loitering on the beaches
Boys whose wandering poisons the evenings.
They no longer hear the language they speak
They weep like dogs
Watching the moon fall
Into the horizon that bathes me.
They devour their own flesh
And make love then lacerate their cocks
With their eyes closed for they had no more desires.
They dance amid the jostled universe
The frantic dance of scalped hopes…

Are *they* then my fellow creatures?
And Lord am I on the same waves
Wallowing like a gravid sow
On pestilential tripe,
Shaken by rumbling bowels
I thought were suave ropes
In the flank of a hypertrophied heart
Beating an angelic tomtom? Am I
To slip as far down as the womb
Shut jewel-case where time awaits
Endlessly the completion
Of things?

BLUES

La voie du chemin de fer me lie à ces jours d'enfer
La voie du chemin de fer une seule nuit peut tout faire

Amour des autres tu m'uses à grands coups de brosse dure

Dans une gare de Paris est-ce l'amour qui sourit?
Dans une gare de de Paris tout commence et tout finit.

Amour des autres tu suces le jeune sang de ma vie

Et les mots de mon grand frère que j'entends encore dans mon lit
Et les mots de mon grand frère se peut-il qu'il les oublie?

Amour des autres tu tardes à promettre récompense.

Ainsi soit-il mon enfant y en a qui sont pas contents
Ainsi soit-il mon enfant on gagne on perd tout le temps

Amour des autres tu crèves mes yeux à force de fièvres.

Adieu c'est un grand mouchoir un grand mouchoir de papier
Qu'on jette à l'égout après que les larmes l'ont souillé.

Amour des autres tu laisses dans la bouche un goût de glaise.

BLUES

The bed of the railway links me to these days of hell
The bed of the railway just one night can do it all

Love of the others you wear me out with great strokes of a stiff brush

In a station of Paris is there a true love that smiles?
In a station of Paris everything begins and everything fails.

Love of the others you suck the young blood of my life

And the words of my big brother I still hear them on my cot
And the words of my big brother can it be he forgot?

Love of the others you are slow to promise a reward.

So be it my child some people are never satisfied
So be it my child some win some fall by the wayside

Love of the others you put out my eyes by dint of fevers.

Goodbye is a big handkerchief a big handkerchief of paper
That you throw in the sewer once it's been soiled with tears

Love of the others you leave in my mouth a taste of clay.

QUATORZE MILLIONS D'ANNEES-LUMIERE

Oubliés tout à l'heure et demain
Eclate dans un bruit que nulle oreille ne perçoit
Le commencement de la fin
Puisque tout ce qui commence finit
L'univers comme une ligne comme ce poème une vie
Connaître son père et sa mère et leurs pères

Savoir qu'au plus lointain calendrier
Le corps d'un animal si monocellulaire
Qu'il n'a laissé de trace dans les couches profondes
Se trouve attiré par son semblable,
Qu'il a fallu être deux pour être un...

Love-toi près de moi mon ventre épouse ton dos
Une autre nuit défilera quand nous dormons
Et si nous dormons quelle nuit infinie
Où nulle question ne sera posée
Nulle théorie ne surgira de nos songes?

Tiens ma main rejoignons ensemble
L'oubli de l'heure et de demain
Du grand commencement de toutes choses qui finissent
Corps flagellé oeuf unis dans la nuit infinie
Toute vérité pourrait nourrir nos mensonges
Love-toi près de moi dormons ensemble.

FOURTEEN MILLION LIGHT-YEARS

Now that See you later and tomorrow are forgotten
The beginning of the end
Explodes into a sound that no ear perceives
Since everything that begins ends
The universe like a line like this poem a life
To know one's father and one's mother and their fathers

To know that on the farthest calendar
The body of an animal so monocellular that it
Left no trace in the deep strata
Finds itself attracted to its fellow,
To know that it was necessary to be two in order to be one…

Coil up next to me my stomach fits your back
Another night will pass while we sleep
And if we sleep what infinite night
Wherein no question will be asked
No theory rise out of our dreams.

Hold my hand let's go back together
To the forgetting of the hour and tomorrow
Of the great beginning of all things that end
Flagellar body joined with the egg in endless darkness
Every truth could nurture our lies
Coil up next to me let's sleep together.

APRES L'ORAGE

Maintenant pour partir
La lune est trop bas.
On atteint la plage à la marche
Une heure passée avec les tarots
A cassé le jour en deux miroirs
Images mouillées racines dénudées
Chevelures offertes aux dernières
Goulées du vent liant les mains.

Assise la frileuse au feu de sa croix
Attend que la nuit la saisisse.
Les roseaux chuintent mâts scintillants.
Dans le portefeuille parmi les photos de noyés
Décapité par les myriapodes,
Un loup se transforme en soupirs
Ainsi parfois dans la forêt pleurent
Les lionnes un psaume, un mot perdus.

Le cri au retour de l'oiseau
Annonce d'épaisses rencontres
Alors la langue que percent les dents
Ne demande plus quel chemin conduit
Au sable abreuvé de salive.
Le coeur sèche avec le rivage.
L'espoir s'engloutit dans la nuit.
La lune monte l'implacable.

AFTER THE STORM

Now the moon is too low
For us to leave
We get to the beach on foot
An hour spent with the tarot cards
Has broken the day into two mirrors
Wet images roots laid bare
Tresses offered to the last
Mouthfuls of wind tying our hands together.

The woman sitting by the fire of her cross feels cold
Waits for night to seize her.
Reeds shushing masts sparkling.
In the wallet amid photos of drowned people
Decapitated by centipedes and millipedes,
A wolf transforms himself into sighs
So sometimes in the forest lionesses
Weep for a lost psalm, a lost word.

The cry at the bird's return
Announces thick encounters
It's then that the tongue pierced by teeth
No longer asks which road leads
To the sand slaked with saliva.
The heart dries out with the shore.
Hope sinks into night.
The moon the implacable rises.

DIAMANT NOIR

La paisible harmonie d'un dimanche matin
Plein des couleurs d'un apparent silence,
Le paysage dehors vert et bleu, le soleil
Caché derrière l'occasionnel carillon d'une église
Et dans la chambre une présence qui s'en va,
Un au revoir flottant dans l'air comme
Le dernier ruban d'une fumée de cigarette…

La porte fermée on se retrouve devant la mer
Miroir qui ne reflète ni la fenêtre ni le monde
Brutalement impénétrable où l'on peut peindre toutefois
L'obscur le fulgurant et les deux infinis
Les musiques les mots l'irréel et le vrai
Le souffle de la vie éphémère buée
Le coeur brûlant brûlé aux feux d'un diamant noir.

Il y a un lit dans toutes nos journées
Une chute soudaine, une difficile descente.
Toujours autant de jours que nous vivons
Dans l'heure où nous quittons le jour, pour commencer
L'apprentissage jamais accompli de la nuit.

Stagnent dans ce loisir de notre veille d'autres
Tableaux qui nous égarent, paysages rompus, visages
Oubliés et les monstres de nos précédentes rencontres
Avec les images que nous renvoie le mur de notre chambre
Face à la fenêtre dont il n'est pas le reflet.

Le jardin clos d'iris et de roses de Sharon
L'eau du bassin où s'ébroue le gras rouge-gorge
Le sifflet du train, la campagne jusqu'au fleuve
La pleine lune et ses tourbillons de nuée bleues
Toute la terre et nous seuls à savoir que nous dormons
Toujours seuls, une fois les paupières fermées,
Et le néant qui achèvera de durer…

BLACK DIAMOND

The peaceful harmony of a Sunday morning
Filled with the colors of an apparent silence,
The landscape outside green and blue, the sun
Hidden behind the occasional chiming from a church
And in the bedroom a presence that is leaving,
A goodbye floating in the air like
The last ribbon of cigarette smoke...

Once the door has shut one is back before the sea
Mirror that reflects neither the window nor the world
Brutally impenetrable where one can nonetheless paint
The dark the flashing and the two infinities
The musics the words the unreal and the true
The breath of life fleeting vapor
The burning heart burnt in the sparkle of a black diamond.

There is a bed in all our days
A sudden fall, a difficult descent
Always as many days as we live
In the hour when we leave day to begin the never finished
Apprenticeship of night.

Stagnating in this leisure of our vigil other
Pictures that lose us, broken landscapes, forgotten
Faces and the monsters of our previous meetings
With the images the bedroom wall beams back to us
Facing the window of which it is not the reflection.

The enclosed garden of iris and roses of Sharon
The water in the birdbath where the fat robin fusses
The train whistle, the country down to the river
The full moon and its eddies of blue cloud
All the earth and only we to know that we sleep
Always alone, once our eyelids are shut,
And the nothingness which will leave off lasting...

CAPSULE

War ein Haus wo, da warst du drein
Und die Leute schicken mich herein.
Hugo von Hofmannsthal
—Der Rosenkavalier

J'essayai désespérement de penser à quelque chose
Qui ne m'était encore jamais venu a l'esprit
Et ce fut d'entrer dans un tube d'aluminium
Comprimé d'aspirine ou cigare. Je me desséchais
N'attendant plus la pluie dans cet espace confiné —
Situation étrange mais on en voit de pire
Dans les films d'horreur.
                              Or il plut. Il suffisait
D'y croire avec force, une fois entré dans la tube.
Of course!
              Vous ignorerez toujours la puissance
Et la résistance du vouloir avant de sentir
Comme une lézarde dans l'air comprimé autour de vous
L'air lui-même comme un mur. Le jour comme une lézarde
Au fond d'un puits. Et que ce que vous preniez
Pour une vague sur quoi rouler votre paresse,
Comme dans l'abime minuscule fragment, une cloche à plongeur.
Oui. Au commencement est la lézarde
L'échelle. Puis l'effort pour deviner si l'on est
A la surface de la paroi ou sous la cloche.
Ding ding dong. C'est le même son.
Vous vous balancez au fanon d'Apis
Vous vous desséchez dans la capsule d'aluminium
Vous attendez désespérement la pluie
La moindre goutte de changement.

CAPSULE

War ein Haus wo, da warst du drein
Und die Leute schicken mich herein.
                Hugo von Hofmannsthal
                    —Der Rosenkavalier

I was trying desperately to think of something
That had never occurred to me before
And it was to enter an aluminum tube
Like the ones for aspirin or cigars. I was drying up,
No longer expecting rain in that narrow space —
Curious situation but you see worse ones
In horror movies.
                Well, it was raining. It was enough
To believe it, forcefully, once I was inside the tube.
Of course!
                You'll never know the power
And the resistance of the will until you feel
Like a crevice in the compressed air around you
The air itself like a wall. Daylight like a crevice
At the bottom of a well. And what you mistook
For a wave on which to roll your laziness,
A diving bell, minuscule fragment in the abyss.
Yes. In the beginning is the crevice
The ladder. Then the effort to find out if one is
On the surface of the partition or under the bell.
Ding ding dong. It's the same sound.
You dangle from the dewlap of Apis
You dry out in the aluminum capsule
You wait desperately for rain
The least drop of change.

LAC ROUGE ET NOIR

Poème démodé

Fulgurences silencieuses échappant au temps
Rubans de lumière soudain donnant vie aux ténèbres
A l'horizon griffées d'éclairs, et sur les vagues dont la présence
Se trahissait par un humide clapotis aveuglante
Etendue obscure alourdie de caoutchouc d'huiles visqueux
Commencements sans témoins du monde

Une à une les voitures s'arrêtent feux éteints
Radios fermés. On n'entend pas les oiseaux dit une femme
On n'entend pas le tonnerre c'est curieux dit un homme
Il cherche la main rassurante d'un enfant
Ils avancent sur la plage herbeuse
Il me semble qu'il fait froid dit un vieillard

Et peu à peu mais à la vitesse d'un songe
S'embrase le panorama jusqu'à révéler
De grands pans de paysage sur la rive lointaine
Tels qu'on ne les vit jamais par le jour le plus clair
Qui disparaissent et renaissent dans le grondement
Continu comme d'une bête qui s'éveille

Les déchirures de néant le flamboiement des eaux
Le crépitement différé de gigantesques étincelles
La couleur révélée du ciel en feu
Le bruit l'odeur de l'eau agitée
Et le tonitruant vacarme coupé
De brefs silences électriques

L'orage roule sur le lac le lac rougeoie
Le monde croule de nuées noires
Le vent qui se lève rabat les voix
De grosses gouttes claquent sur les pare-brise
Puis la pluie se déchaine en longues draperies
Qui se retroussent sur l'asphalte au feu des phares

RED AND BLACK LAKE

Old-fashioned poem

Silent flashes escaping from time
Ribbons of light suddenly bringing the shadows to life
On the horizon scrawled with lightning, and on the
        waves whose presence
Is revealed by a damp blinding plashing
Dim expanse weighted with rubber with viscous oils
Unwitnessed beginnings of the world

One by one the cars stop their lights off
Their radios off. You don't hear the birds says a woman
You don't hear the thunder it's strange says a man
He reaches for a child's reassuring hand
They move forward on the grassy beach
It seems to me that it's cold says an old man

And little by little but at the speed of a dream
The panorama catches fire until it reveals
Enormous landscape panels on the distant shore
As one never saw them before in brightest daylight
That disappear and are reborn in the continual
Growling like that of an animal waking

The rents in nothingness the flaming of the waters
The deferred sputtering of gigantic sparks
The revealed color of the fiery sky
The sound the smell of the churning water
And the thundering racket cut
By brief electric silences

The storm rolls on the lake the lake reddens
The world collapses from black clouds
The rising wind beats down the voices
Big drops slap the windshield
Then the rain breaks loose in long curtains
That tuck themselves up from the asphalt in the glare
        of the headlights

PELE-MELE

Une voix qui dit: "Vous l'avez voulu"
Et la même chambre au matin suivant.

Une autre qui dit: "Il ne fallait pas"
Et sa résonnance au cours des années.

Un enfant qui dit: "Je ne puis aimer"
Un adulte écoute et ne comprend pas.

Un soldat qui pleure au bord d'un oued
Un autre qui rit en mourant pour rien.

La lettre à portée des regards curieux
Qui n'apprenait rien qu'on ne sût déjà.

Un après-midi de quatorze juillet
Ce feu d'artifice au-dessous des toits.

Un train de minuit pour Dieppe et Le Havre
Et deux innocents rêvant l'Amérique.

En hâte avalées aspirine hostie
Et ce mal de coeur qui n'en finit pas.

La foule en liesse un rapide adieu
Un mot souligné dans le dictionnaire.

L'escalier rayon des coeurs esseulés
L'appel d'un regard qu'on ne verra plus.

Ternis sous la poussière et la vitre salie,
Rendus précieux par ces éclairs de la mémoire,
Je vous contemple instants de mes heurs et malheurs,
Trop pauvre que je suis pour dédaigner si peu.

PELL-MELL

A voice that says: "You wanted it this way"
And the same room the next morning.

Another that says: "You shouldn't have"
And its resonance through the years.

A child who says: "I don't know how to love"
An adult listens and doesn't understand.

A soldier who weeps beside a wadi
Another who laughs, dying for nothing.

The letter within plain sight of inquisitive eyes
That told nothing that wasn't already known.

An afternoon of quatorze juillet
That fireworks display below the roofs.

A midnight train for Dieppe and Le Havre
And two innocents dreaming America.

Aspirin eucharist swallowed in haste
And that nausea that never ends.

The enraptured crowd a rapid farewell
A word underlined in the dictionary.

The stairway lonely hearts department
The urging of a gaze one will not see again.

Tarnished under dust and behind dirty glass,
Gilded by the lightning of memory,
I consider you, moments of my happiness and distress,
Being too poor to disdain so little.

L'HEURE QU'IL EST

"Ne descendez pas trop" dit-elle. "En bas
On s'écrase comme punaises sous la semelle.
Sentez-vous la puanteur qui épaissait
Sur la langue le goût de l'air?"
L'homme dardé de flèches défraichies
Laissa comme un regret le bord de l'abîme de boue.
Il avait tant rêvé d'aller voir comment grouillent
Les cohortes semblables à ses fantasmes
Qui copulent au plis de ses nuits
Se reproduisent en progression érotique
Et finissent par s'endormir
Repus d'abjection satisfaite
Prêts à crever pour prix de leurs délices.

"N'insistez pas" dit-elle. "Il sera temps
Quand leur petite machine programmée pour ces exploits
Cessera sa course sur les parois de l'égout
Quand l'air méphitique se fera rare à leurs poumons
D'aller noter sur les faces à l'agonie
Quels interdits ils ont enfreints quelle
Facette de la nuit ils n'ont pas su
Distinguer dans leur frénésie quel
Monstre ils n'ont pas vu que cachait le temps."
L'homme bardé d'impatience irraisonnée
Se laissa glisser lentement vers l'abîme
L'oeil fixé sur sa montre. "Il est l'heure" dit-il
"De connaître par moi-même ce qu'est la vie."

WHAT TIME IT IS

"Don't go down too far," she said, "Down there
They're getting crushed like bedbugs under someone's shoes
Don't you smell the stench that thickens
The taste of the air on your tongue?"
The man pierced with shopworn arrows
Left behind like a regret the brink of the abyss of mud.
He had been so eager to see the swarming
Of cohorts that might have resembled his phantasms,
That copulate in the folds of nights
Reproduce in an erotic progression,
And end by falling asleep
Glutted with abject satisfactions,
Ready to burst as the price of their delectations.

"Don't insist," she said. "There will be time
Enough when their little machine, programmed for these exploits,
Will cease to run around the brim of the sewer,
When the mephitic air will grow thin in their lungs,
To go and observe the death-agony on their faces —
What interdicts they infringed what
Facet of the night they weren't able
To distinguish in their frenzy what
Monsters hidden by time they failed to see."
The man encased in unreasonable impatience
Let himself slide slowly toward the abyss,
His eye fixed on his watch. "It's time," he said,
"To go see for myself what life is."

UNE VEUVE

Des fontaines s'allumaient sous nos pas ce soir-là
Des colonnes supportaient les châteaux inaccessibles
Ce soir-là. Le ciel mauve illuminait d'orages
Devant des mille-fleurs les vénéneux cattleyas.

Comment va-t-on au pied des tours jumelles?
On n'y va pas. Les tours ont étouffé les rues.
Rien ne conduit alors au fleuve sous ses ponts?
Une ville reconnue nous rapproche d'hier.

Devant un lion de pierre au blason émoussé
Debout, était-ce moi? Mon ombre à ses genoux pliée
Etait-ce lui? La fenêtre donnait sur la gare
Le néon balbutiait un temps semblable au temps.

Enfin réconciliés entre bonsoir et baiser
Entre hier et demain qui suspend l'insomnie
Nous avons découvert notre première nuit
Oubliant le regret des chambres séparées.

Comment va-t'on aux douves feuillues aux remparts?
On n'y va plus. Les tours rasées ont comblé le fossé
Un adieu s'est noué au fil des voies ferrées
Le jour a retrouvé ses contours oubliés.

Dans un désert d'obstacles et d'objets désolés
Vivante était-ce moi clouée à la trace de rêves
Pleurant ces mains nouées qu'un départ a tranchées
Moi qu'alourdit le deuil d'un bonheur oublié?

A WIDOW

Fountains came alight under our feet that evening
Columns supported inaccessible castles
That evening. The violet sky lit storms
Of blossoming fireworks behind the poisonous cattleyas.

How does one get to the foot of the twin towers?
One doesn't. The towers have stifled the streets.
Then nothing leads to the river under the bridges?
A recognized city reproaches us with yesterday.

In front of a stone lion with a mossy coat-of-arms
Was it me, standing? My shadow bent at his knees
Was it him? The window gave on the station
The neon stammered a weather that was like the weather.

Reconciled at last between goodnight and kisses
Between yesterday and tomorrow which defers insomnia
We discovered our first night
Forgetting the regret of separate bedrooms.

How does one get to the leafy moats at the ramparts?
One doesn't anymore. The razed towers have filled the ditch
A farewell tied itself to the wire of the railway
Day rediscovered its forgotten contours.

In a desert of obstacles and desolate objects
Was it me alive nailed to the trace of dreams
Weeping for my bound hands that a departure has cut off
Me weighted with mourning a forgotten happiness?

RIEN A DIRE

Porte ouverte sur rien à dire
Chambre réelle clair tombeau
Je meurs je vis murs éclatés éblouisssante
Lumière cours fracassant du temps
L'histoire s'attache à mes membres
Je vis je rêve entre ses rives
Gravées d'innombrables annales
Autre tombe d'éternité
Table de bronze où l'on dissèque
Parmi les idées écaillées
Mon corps irradiant ses folies
Au front fêlé d'un dieu qui ne se connaît pas
Et qui pourtant devrait connaître
Pourquoi cette porte est béante
Pourquoi la chambre ouverte donne
Sur le tombeau sur rien à dire.

NOTHING TO SAY

Door open on nothing to say
Actual bedroom daylit tomb
I die I live burst walls blinding
Light splintering flow of time
History sticks to my limbs
I live I dream between its banks
Graven with innumerable annals
Another tomb of eternity
Bronze table where they dissect
Among flaking ideas
My body radiating its madness
To the cracked forehead of a god
Who doesn't recognize himself
But who still ought to know why
This door is gaping
Why the open bedroom gives on
The tomb, on nothing to say.

TROIS PETITS POEMES

I

Un pays différent du nôtre
meurt sur les doigts d'un
feu de bois. Le ciel se
couche alors sur moi et le
soleil me prend la bouche.

Contrée, tes arbres sont
entrés l'un dans l'autre
et nos mains jointes créent
un royaume où se perdre est
se retrouver.

II

Aux attaches des plus précieuses
parures stagne le temps qui garde
toute moiteur jusqu'à ce que ton
corps y nage remontant ses propres
rigueurs.
            Les eaux premières à la
source composent selon le nouvel
ordre et le prochain reflet un
cours dont les méandres touchent
tout instant pour mieux l'émouvoir

Ainsi s'étale un lit que le ciel
ignorait où gisent le fugace et
l'instable dans le cheminement de
rares géographies.

THREE LITTLE POEMS

I

A country different from ours
dies on the fingers of a
wood fire. The sky then
sets on me and the
sun takes my mouth.

Land, your trees have
entered one another
and our joined hands create
a kingdom where being lost
is being found.

II

At the clasp of the most precious
sets of jewelry stagnates the climate that
keeps all its clamminess until your
body swims upstream against its own
rigors.
　　　　The first waters at the
spring compose according to the
new rule and the next reflection
a stream whose meanders touch
each instant the better to excite it

Thus a bed sprawls that the sun
didn't know about, wherein lie the fleeting
and the unstable in the advancing of
rare geographies.

III

Nuit réduite à la ligne nue où
se joignent les paupières quand
la lampe et son jour faux cessent
de meurtrir nos yeux.
                            Derrière
tu vois l'écran des apparences
conservées les modulations du
néant l'échappatoire inconscient.

III

Night reduced to the naked line where
the   eyelids   join   when
the lamp and its false daylight cease
to   bruise   our   eyes.
                                    Behind
you   see   the   screen   of   kept-up
appearances   the   modulations   of
nothingness the unconscious loophole.

TOTEN INSEL

La voix connue, un vieil ami m'arrache aux délices du port
Et tandis que nous remontons ensemble vers le bois de myrte:
"Dis moi, dit-il, prenant ma main comme au temps de nos promenades,
Pourquoi tu arrives déjà et comment tu fis le chemin.
A cette heure-ci les bureaux sont fermés...
On peut d'ailleurs attendre aussi longtemps qu'on veut avant d'entrer...
Impossible de se perdre, inutile de s'inquiéter.
On peut aussi se promener si on le désire
Aussi longtemps qu'on le désire."

Et moi, me retournant, je ne vois plus rien sur l'autre bord
Qu'un pan doré de brumes, qu'îles avec des photographies reflétées,
Et les mâtures, les bateaux, les branches d'arbres calcinéees,
Quelque chose comme un adieu figé entre le ciel et l'eau.

C'est pire que prévu mais le pire était prévu.

Si encore, j'étais sûr
D'être ici
De vous avoir retrouvés
De parler
Et d'éprouver avec vous
Des regrets...

Les maisons se ressemblent toutes
Des fleurs séchées parmi le sable des allées.
D'une terrasse à l'autre un téléphone permettrait...
Mais est-ce bien la même maison et n'y a-t-il pas
D'océan entre les îles rendant toute conversation impossible
Parce qu'il pleut? Surtout que... parlons nous vraiment la même
    langue?

J'ai commencé à perdre espoir un soir
Lorsque cherchant encore à croire à une aurore
Je savais que le jour glisserait hors de la nuit
             Sans moi,
Effleurant les arbres les antennes les corniches
Et toucherait, à travers la vitre, mon visage

TOTEN INSEL

The familiar voice, an old friend plucks me from the harbor's delights
And as we climb together toward the myrtle wood:
"Tell me," he says, taking my hand as in the time of our excursions,
"Why you arrive so soon, and how you journeyed.
At this hour the offices are closed...
Besides, you can wait as long as you like without going in...
It's impossible to get lost, and pointless to worry.
Or we can go for a walk, if you wish,
For as long as you wish."

And turning, I no longer see anything on the other shore,
Nothing but a gilded patch of fog, islands, with reflected photographs,
And the masts and spars, the boats, the charred branches of trees,
Something like a goodbye frozen between the sky and the water.

It's worse than predicted, but the worst was predicted.

Yet if only I was sure
Of being here,
Of having found you all again
Of speaking
And of feeling regret
With you...

The houses all look alike:
Dried flowers along the sandy walks.
From one terrace to another a telephone would allow...
But is this really the same house and isn't there
Ocean among the islands making all conversation impossible
Because it's raining? Especially since... are we really speaking the
    same language?

I began to lose hope one evening
When, still trying to believe in a dawn,
I knew that day would slide out of night,
            Without me,
Grazing the trees the antennas the cornices
And would touch, through the pane, my covered

Couvert, ayant accepté le poids du drap, moi qui
A la moindre main près de mon sommeil m'éveillais.
C'était donc l'aube où je devrais nâitre à jamais,
Que j'avais tant redoutée, m'attendant
A des convulsions des éclats de sanie sur les murs
A des horreurs hurlées.

        Mais:
J'étais seulement debout devant un magasin d'autographes.
Sous une vitre, une lettre dont mon reflet cachait les lignes
Adressée à moi était à vendre. Et j'ai glissé
Sur le trottoir comme une serviette mouillée...

        Ou bien
J'écoutais après un court diner après l'amour,
L'autre à peine parti, son odeur à mes doigts,
Mon coeur ralentir tout à coup puis sursauter
Et se taire...

        Ou bien
J'entrais en un rêve et croyais y courir
Après un enfant nu que cachaient les buissons
Et qui, passant à gué une rivière,
Tout emperlé de gouttelettes d'arc-en-ciel
De la rive adverse en chantant exaltait
La tiédeur de sa main le chaud de son aisselle
Le velours de son flanc ou ses armes.
Et j'étouffais en me noyant dans les rapides...

J'avais appris la joie, la vie, parmi de jeunes fous,
Colibris colorés dansant autour de moi.
Dans un jardin pailleté, sous des arches en feuillées,
Une licorne assise aux feux des cheminées
Pâle, lustrait sa croupe, seins dardés,
Platon ouvert devant des carafes vidées
Et sur le mur une ombre une horloge figée
Moi qui entre, moi qui refuse de me perdre
Parmi toutes délices escomptées.

Cherchais-je une fontaine ou bien l'oubli
Un astrolabe ou l'équipage d'un galion
Pour boire avec moi à ma soif?

Face, which had accepted the weight of the sheet, I who
Used to waken at the slightest hand near my sleep.
So it was the dawn when I was to be born forever,
That I had dreaded so much, expecting
Convulsions, shards of pus on the walls,
Shouted horrors.
                    But:
I was only standing in front of an autograph shop.
Under glass, where my reflection hid the lines,
A letter addressed to me was for sale,
And I slipped on the sidewalk like a wet towel...
                    Or else
I was listening — after a brief dinner, after love,
The other had barely left, his smell still on my fingers —
To my heart slacken all at once, then start
And fall silent...
                    Or else
I was entering a dream where I thought I ran
After a naked child screened by bushes
Who, fording a river,
Beaded with rainbow drops,
Singing from the opposite bank, intensified
The warmth of his hand, the heat of his armpit,
The down of his side or his weapons.
And I choked, drowning in the rapids...

I had learned joy, life, among young madmen,
Colored hummingbirds dancing around me.
In a spangled garden, under leafy arches,
A unicorn seated by the fires of the fireplaces,
Pale, polished its flank, its breasts pointed,
Plato open before the emptied flasks
And on the wall a shadow a congealed clock
Me going in, me who refuses to lose me
Among all anticipated pleasures.

Was I looking for a fountain or was it oblivion
An astrolabe or the crew of a galleon
To drink with me to my thirst?

Des pigeons polluaient l'eau du lac
A moins que ce ne fut une ombelle tombée
A moins que ce ne fussent phrases mal réglées:
"Nos bicyclettes renversées sur les zinnias…"
Où allais-je sans autre carte qu'un miroir?
Chaque visage au soir jaillissait du cambouis
Comme une insulte à un appareil génital
Et les yeux regardaient qui les regarde
Vaciller, tenir à distance, tandis que
La beauté battait le tambour aux fenêtres:
Chambres scellées personne pour crier au feu!
Alors je vis passer quelqu'un au pied du lit
Sans savoir si c'était moi ou personne.
La lampe brillait sans courant.
Le dos des livres parlait une langue indécise
Les bruits de la rue ne rapprochaient plus les charrois familiers.
Je prenais une main qui ne palpitait plus.
Je sifflais, et des voix frileuses emmitouflées
Ne répondaient pas à leur nom pourtant hurlé
Comme si elles étaient sourdes.
Ou mortes.

Je tourne autour du silence.
Le puits sans profondeur n'a plus d'eau pour ma soif.
La je m'abîme, néant discret,
Là où imperceptiblement m'a conduit ma vie.
Là je tombe
Ayant toujours ignoré tout pourquoi.
Mais les jours et les nuits de ma quête,
Qui les a contemplés, témoin glacé, sans voir
Qu'une flamme dormait au tréfonds de mon sang?
Les livres lus de compagnie
Les musiques et les musées
Les paysages habités
M'auront laissé seul.
Et le ciel même où je ne retrouve pas
La couleur durable du temps
Tourne n'importe comment, toutes étoiles brouillées,
Si confusément que je crois marcher droit

Pigeons polluted the lake water
Unless it was a fallen umbel,
Unless it was badly worded phrases:
"Our bicycles overturned on the zinnias…"
Where was I going with no other map than a mirror?
At evening each face shot up out of the motor oil
Like an insult to a genital organ
And the eyes looked at who watches them
Vacillate, keeping a distance, while
Beauty beat the drum at the windows:
The rooms sealed, no one to cry "Fire!"
Then I saw someone pass the foot of the bed,
Not knowing if it was myself or no one.
The lamp glowed without electric current.
The spines of books spoke an imprecise language,
The sounds of the street no longer brought the familiar carts closer.
I pressed a hand that no longer palpitated.
I whistled, and chilly muffled voices
Didn't answer to their name, though it was shouted.
As though they were deaf.
Or dead.

I hang around silence.
The depthless well has no more water for my thirst.
There, I am swallowed up, discreet nothingness,
There where my life has imperceptibly led me.
There, I fall
Having never known any why.
But the days and nights of my search,
Who has gazed on them, a frozen witness, without seeing
That a flame slept in the deepest strata of my blood?
The books read in company,
The musics and museums
The inhabited landscapes
Will have left me alone.
And even the sky, where I no longer find
The lasting color of the weather,
Turns every which way, all stars scrambled,
So vaguely that I think I'm walking straight

Dans un monde aux itinéraires fermés,
Sang sur lui-même bouclé
Cercle des méridiens sans fin.
Si peu de jours rattrapant le temps donné…
Et si peu de mots repétés par tant de bouches
Maintenant que je commence à n'être rien.

"Inutile de s'inquiéter
Impossible de se perdre
On peut toujours se promener si on le désire
Aussi longtemps qu'on le désire…"

In a world of closed circuits,
Blood coiled on itself
Encircles endless meridians.
So few days overtaking the time that is given...
And so few words repeated by so many mouths
Now that I'm beginning to be nothing.

"It's pointless to worry
Impossible to get lost,
We can go for a walk if you wish,
For as long as you wish..."

TOUTES LES QUESTIONS SAUF UNE

Le public est libre de poser
Toutes les questions
    Sauf une
Sous peine de disparaître
    Dans la trappe
Ouverte par le meneur de jeu
    Un homme gras
Masqué de papier journal enflammé.

Je puis commencer ma prière in petto
Et finir par recevoir
Un morceau de sucre sur la langue
Pour arriver — dans quel état —
A la tranche des galaxies.
Nuit de quatorze juillet pleine de gloire
    Et découvrir
Qu'il y a d'autres découvertes à faire.

L'étincelle d'absence
Contenue dans le temps
Le chemin à l'envers
Vers l'explosion originelle
Et derrière l'homme au masque
Quelle imposture voilée
Elle aussi pour interdire
De savoir quoi demander.
    A qui?

Il faudrait recommencer la séance
Avec d'autres spectateurs
Briser toutes les idoles
Sans en dresser de nouvelles
Et si nous trouvons l'être au masque
Celui qui n'existe pas
Transgresser nos angoisses
Et lui casser la gueule.
    Peut-être....

EVERY QUESTION BUT ONE

The audience is free to ask
Every question
        But one
On pain of disappearing
        Through the trapdoor
Opened by the master of ceremonies
        A heavy man
Masked with flaming newsprint.

I can start my prayer *in petto*
And end by receiving
A lump of sugar on my tongue
To arrive — but in what condition! —
At the cut edge of the galaxies
The night of July fourteenth full of glory
        And discover
That there are other discoveries to make.

The spark of absence
Contained in time
The road backward
Toward the original explosion
And behind the man with the mask
What veiled trickery
Is also there to forbid
Knowing what to ask for?
        Of whom?

We would have to start the performance again
With other spectators
Smash all the idols
Without erecting new ones
And if we found the creature with the mask
The one who doesn't exist
Disobey our anxieties
And smash his face.
        Perhaps....

PASSANT LA FRONTIERE

La ligne se voyait depuis
Longtemps au gré de la route
Et si l'on s'endormait au volant
Fulgurait dans l'âme assoupie
Comme une révélation brutale
Qui vous évitait de sentir
Dans l'instantané onirique
Votre cervelle s'écraser
Sur la borne ou le pare-brise

C'était une ligne idéale
Sommée de bleu horizontal
Qui déployait jour aprés jour
Comme la corde d'une lessive
Drapeaux et scalps et roses délavés
Nos pays nos combats nos guerres
Mêlant lassitude et sursauts
Une gymnastique en désordre
Qui rendait malade nos coeurs

PASSING THE FRONTIER

The yellow line could be seen for as long a time
As the highway desired
And if you fell asleep at the wheel
It fulgurated in the dozing soul
Like a brutal revelation
That allowed you not to feel
In the dream's snapshot
Your brain getting smashed
Against the milestone or the windshield

It was an ideal line
Crowned with horizontal blue
That unwound day after day
Like a clothesline
Flags and scalps and washed-out roses
Our countries our combats our wars
Mingling lassitude with involuntary starts
A gymnastic in disorder
That sickened our hearts

GANYMEDE

Un mur, un miroir: c'est le ciel, n'est-ce pas?

Par les éclats du jour entre l'hélicoptère.
Il enlève dans ses serres un clerc endormi,
L'emporte par des corridors aseptisés
Jusqu'à l'Olympe où règne — parmi l'acier,
Les horoscopes, les hormones, les ordures —
Vieille première communiante violée,
La Ville, enrubannée de méphitiques nuées.

C'est ici, enfin, que tout s'explique:

"…Je viens d'une ferme où le tabac croît
Sous un velum impénétrable aux bactéries…
Là, dans un hallier touffu de feuilles molles
Que sur sa cuisse nue une nymphe écrasait,
J'ai grandi, par moi-même à moi-même enchainé…"

"…Une yole fendait le lac un jour de pluie,
Tirée par de gros gars oints de suif, leurs mains
Cousues pour écarter les tentations,
Jusqu'à la rive adverse empoisonnée de lierre…"

"…J'ai lu la Bible entre des herbes stupéfiantes
Et Saint François dans un bol de lait bleu…"

"…J'ai voulu mourir à bicyclette mais midi
N'a pas duré assez longtemps pour me percer…"

"…Un matin traversé d'orages magnétiques,
Le ventre creux, j'ai monté, descendu sans fin
Un escalier glacé au flanc d'un gâteau d'anges…"

C'est tout. Le reste a pris plus de temps
A passer qu'à demeurer dans ma mémoire.
Et maintenant, pressé sous le poids du béton
Je sue lentement, par tous les sphincters, l'ennui.
Cela dépend du ciel, des plaisirs collectifs,
De la douleur, des auréoles, des capsules.

GANYMEDE

A wall, a mirror: it's the sky, isn't it?

Through the shards of the day the helicopter enters.
It seizes a sleeping clerk in its claws,
Carries him off through antiseptic corridors
To Olympus, where amid steel, horoscopes, hormones,
Garbage, the City — ribboned with mephitic thunderheads:
An old, violated first communicant — rules.

It's here, finally, that everything is explained:

"...I come from a farm where tobacco grows
Under an awning bacteria cannot penetrate...
There in a dense thicket of soft leaves
That a nymph crushed against her naked thigh,
I grew up, chained by myself to myself..."

"...A yawl cleaved the lake one rainy day
Drawn by big guys smeared with suet, their hands
Sewn shut to avoid temptations
As far as the opposite shore, poisoned with ivy..."

"...I read the Bible amid narcotic herbs
And St. Francis in a bowl of blue milk..."

"...I wanted to die on a bicycle but noon
Didn't last long enough to pierce me..."

"...On a morning traversed by electric storms,
On an empty stomach, I climbed, I walked endlessly down
A frozen staircase in the side of an angel's cake..."

That's all. The rest took more time to happen
Than to lodge in my memory.
And now, pressed under the weight of concrete
I sweat boredom slowly, through all my sphincters.
That depends on the sky, on collective pleasures,
On pain, haloes, capsules.

Et les rideaux ne prennent plus feu,
Les phénix se sont coupés les empennures,
Les rhododendrons se ratatinent jusqu'au soir,
Dans le parc, près de flaques
Où se reflètent vos mamelles taries
Grande soeur délavée d'indifférence.
Un vague murmure chlorophyllique demeure,
Lointain brouhaha, toutes portes fermées.

Bientôt c'est la nuit. La Grande Ourse d'avril
Entourée d'îles étincelle.
L'acier d'aujourd'hui fulgure et d'acryliques
Toisons emmaillotent les banknotes.

Je me suis dévêtu sur un rythme syncopé —
Tantôt négresse huilée, tantôt blanche hétaïre
Roses noires à l'aisselle et tintamarre au flanc,
Pour réveiller ces bambins pneumatiques
Leur chyle homogénéisé, leurs ridicules.
Ils frappent sur le clavicorde en kit
Construit après les heures de bureau
La monnaie bidon de Jean-Sébastien Bach,
Absorbée, ingérée, digérée, imprimée
En circuits microscopiques sous leurs lobes.
Maintenant le store à peine tiré devant le permanent
Scintillement des journaux lumineux, des phares,
Difficile de les distraire du Zen, des pilules,
Des vacances vendues en culottes bermudiennes,
Un grand rhum au poing, le couchant flamboyant
A contre-jour dans le duvet de leur jarret.
Difficile de les arracher au poison électronique,
Distillé parmi les déchets industriels,
Aux chiens fous entre les autos, qu'on écrase,
A ce mirage ondoyant de lendemeins plus beaux.
Nous avons essayé la lutte, la contrainte, et
L'abominable persuasion, mes frères et moi.
La croix séchait au pied de notre lit.
La poussière des révolutions avortées
Donnait plus soif encore aux ivrognes roulant
Dans la fange du réel le rêve des hommes.

And the curtains no longer catch fire,
The phoenixes have shorn their plumage,
The rhododendrons shrink until evening.
In the park, near the puddles
Where your dried-up breasts are reflected —
Big sister washed out by indifference.
A vague chlorophyllic murmur stays,
Distant hubbub, all doors shut.

Soon it will be night. The Great Bear of April
Sparkles, surrounded by islands.
The steel of today fulgurates and acrylic
Fleece swaddles the banknotes.

I undressed to a syncopated rhythm —
Sometimes an oiled negress, sometimes a white whore
Black roses at her armpits and noise at her sides,
To waken those pneumatic urchins,
Their homogenized chyle, their ridicule.
On the clavichord built from a kit
After office hours
They strike the counterfeit coins of Johann Sebastian Bach
— Absorbed, ingested, digested, printed
In microscopic circuits under their lobes.
Now with the shade barely raised to reveal the permanent
Glitter of the flashing news-bulletins, the lighthouses,
It's difficult to distract them from Zen, from pills,
From sold vacations in Bermuda shorts —
A large rum in the fist, the sunset blazing
From behind on the down of their shanks.
It's hard to tear them from the electronic poison
Distilled amid industrial waste,
From mad dogs squashed between the cars,
From this wavy mirage of lovelier tomorrows.
We tried struggle, constraint, and
Abominable persuasion, my brothers and I.
The cross dried up at the foot of our bed.
The dust of aborted revolutions
Made the drunks still thirstier as they rolled
The dream of men in the muck of reality.

C'est alors qu'il fallait réapprendre à tourner
Le bois, à tisser l'écorce, à épier le caribou
Les pieds dans des marais gélatineux, seul,
Appuyé sur la lointaine fumée des crépuscules,
A gâcher la science ancestrale avilie
Et chauler la neuve maison.
C'est alors qu'il fallait remonter
Le plus simple jouet pour chanter des merveilles
Et découvrir dans le creux des jours et des nuits
La chaleur des autres. Et l'aimer.
Mais les épis s'étiolent sous la cendre,
D'arrogants bulldozers déciment nos journées,
Arrachent les dolmens, langue coupée le long de la route,
Et de sombres idiots fouillent les tas de feuilles
Mortes sans inventer, sans deviner, sans même voir
L'étincelle sur quoi il suffirait de souffler.
Et quand ils auront fui les moustiques et les herbes,
De grands Indiens, leur pénis peint, leur oeil cerné,
Violeront dans un mirage d'obsidienne
Leurs filles, leurs chevaux et leur rêve d'Indiens.
On retourne à l'histoire racontée aux enfants
Par ces grands loups gris comme n'est plus leur pain.
Les enfants vont encore à l'école aujourd'hui; leur voix,
Orange trop mûre, tombe en plis au pied du drapeau.

Vive les villes verticales
Les piscines au haut des tours
Défi aux hordes de vandales
Durs symboles de faux amours!
Vive les vertes ice-cream
Tournant au rose sous la langue,
Les TV et les limousines,
Les diaphragmes et les amants
Perdus dans les champs d'épandage
Les oiseleurs les assassins
Gravant leur nom dans les écorces
Leur ombre en polaroid!

Olympus, putain chevelue
Dont le nombril électrifié

It's then that we should have learned again to turn
Wood, weave bark, watch for caribou,
Feet in the gelatinous marshes, alone,
Leaning on the distant smoke of twilights,
To spoil the debased ancestral knowledge,
To lime the new house.
It's then we should wind up
The simplest toy to sing of marvels
And discover in the hollows of the days and nights
The heat of others. And to love it.
But the ears of wheat wilt under ash,
Arrogant bulldozers decimate our days,
Rip up the dolmens, tongue cut all along the highways,
And somber idiots burrow in piles of dead leaves
Without inventing, without guessing, without even seeing
The spark on which it would suffice to blow.
And when they will have fled the mosquitoes and the weeds,
Tall Indians with painted penises and rings under their eyes
Will rape in an obsidian mirage
Their daughters, their horses, and their dream of Indians.
We go back to history as it's told to children
By great gray wolves, gray as their bread no longer is.
The children still go to school even today; their voices,
A too-ripe orange, fall in folds at the base of the flag.

Long live vertical cities
Swimming pools on the tops of towers
Challenge to the hordes of vandals
Hard symbols of fake loves!
Long live green ice cream
Turning pink under the tongue,
TV's and limousines
Diaphragms, lovers,
Lost in the sewage farms
Bird catchers and murderers
Carving their names in bark
Their shadows in polaroid!

Mount Olympus great hairy whore
Whose electrified navel

Suinte d'encre et les paupières
S'alourdissent de bismuth
Quand les chats pissent dans les caves
Quand les soldats quittent Beyrouth
Quand les geishas percent leur ventre
Quand les pompiers glissent le long
De perches chromées sexe en mains.
C'est moi qui connais la musique
C'est moi qui écris aux journaux
Qui crie le prix du lait, qui rase
Les jambes paires des Rockettes
C'est moi qui ajoute des ailes
Aux chiens poursuivant l'oncle Tom
Et applaudit aux étincelles
Qui lancent vers la Lune l'homme
Rivé à la chaise élèctrique!

Lequel de vous est vraiment Jupiter?

Oozes ink and whose eyelids
Grow heavy with bismuth
When cats are pissing in cellars
When the soldiers leave Beirut
When geishas pierce their bellies
When firemen slide down the long
Nickel-plated pole prick in hand.
It's I who knows the music
It's I who writes to the newspapers
Who shouts the price of milk, who shaves
The even-numbered legs of Rockettes
It's I who adds wings
To the dogs set on Uncle Tom
And applauds the sparks that send
Moonward the man
Riveted to the electric chair!

Which one of you is really Jupiter?

UNE NUIT SUR LA MER MORTE

Toute chambre est vide
Tout parfum évanoui
Toute présence absente.

Un rideau sépare l'aube
Palme peinte oiseaux silencieux
De la froide nuit intérieure.

L'hotel éteint s'envole vers
Quelque Far-West onirique
Où le cheval monte l'Indien

Où le sable roux des falaises
Se fige en une statue comme
A Sodome la femme de Loth.

Le soleil transparent dessine
Sur la peau sur le sel séché
Des cristaux joyaux improbables

A offir à celle qui chante
Aux rives bitumeuses la
Saison heureuse le sommeil.

A NIGHT ON THE DEAD SEA

Every bedroom is empty
Every perfume vanished
Every presence absent.

A curtain screens the dawn
Painted palm silent birds
From the cold night inside.

The extinct hotel flies away
Toward some oneiric Far West
Where the horse mounts the Indian

Where the reddish sand of the cliffs
Congeals into a statue
Like Lot's wife in Sodom.

The transparent sun traces
On the skin on the dried salt
Crystals improbable jewels

To offer to her
On the bituminous banks,
Who sings of sleep, the fortunate season.

LE PAYSAGISTE

Le grand calme de la mer et des cieux,
L'effroi né des vagues et des nuages —
Miroirs se reflétant eux-mêmes —
Où tourner le regard?
                                Vaut-il mieux
Fermer les yeux et s'absorber
Dans la rumeur intérieure qui refuse
De voir pour mieux faire?
                                Les yeux fermés, donc!
En bas, au ras des flots, montagnes et vallées
Se bousculent et leur double lointain
Limite l'étendue, l'espace, la distance
Sans comparaison possible, sinon là-haut,
Plus mobile écran du soleil, l'errance des nuées.
Les étoiles s'allument sur le noir infini
Trop connu.
                        Le tableau de la nuit
Ne laisse pas de place pour un rêve.
Attendons la véritable nuit.
                                La profondeur
Des yeux clos révèle l'univers en ses abîmes.
A la surface, une prairie enluminée, vert-bleutée
Sans nuance, reçoit, comme une cascade raidie
D'eau vivifiante, les rayons du vrai jour:
Coulée de temps, un peu dure, laser solidifié.
Qu'il faut briser, découper, renvoyer sur elle-même,
Feux de saphir sur feux d'émeraude
Taillant en mille facettes le ciel reflété.
Alors
        abstrait de l'ébloui
                                est tracé
                                        un arbre.
Ce n'est pas un dessin appliqué
Comme celui qui aurait abouti à un brin d'herbe
Courbe harmonieuse sous le poids de la lumière
Si semblable dans son essence, quoiqu'incomparablement
Unique à d'autres brins, peints avec autant d'attention.
Le temps passe. Les ombres tournent,

THE LANDSCAPIST

The great calm of the sea and the skies
The fear born of waves and clouds —
Mirrors reflecting themselves —
Where should we look?
                              Is it better
To shut one's eyes and absorb
Yourself in the inner noise which refuses
To see in order to do better?
                              Eyes shut, then!
Down there, level with the waves, both mountains and valleys
Elbow each other and their far-off replicas
Limit the expanse, the space, the distance
With no possible comparison, unless up there,
More mobile screen of the sun, the odyssey of clouds.
The stars come alight against the too well-known
Infinite dark.
                    The picture of night
Leaves no place for a dream.
Let's wait for the real night.
                              The depth
Of closed eyes reveals the universe in its chasms.
On its surface, an illuminated meadow, matte bluish green,
Receives, like a rigid waterfall
Of vivifying water, rays of the true day:
Time's flow, somewhat hard, solidified laser.
That must be cut up, broken, thrown back on itself,
Flashes of sapphire on emerald flares,
Cutting the reflected sky into a thousand facets.
Then
          abstracted from the dazzle
                              a tree
                                        is traced.
It's not an applied design
Like the one that would have ended in a blade of grass
Harmonious in its bending under the weight of the light
So similar in essence and yet incomparably
Unique next to other blades, painted with the same attention.
Time passes. The shadows turn,

La surface veloutée obscure peu à peu se peuple
D'une myriade — pour peu qu'on les observe à l'échelle requise —
De vies distinctes, mobiles malgré leurs racines,
Eparses dans les ténèbres, sans témoin,
Mais vibrant, épelant de leur miroitement de moire
Une tension hors du vert et du bleu.

Et l'arbre, né de la main, tache panache,
Accident?
        L'arbre échappe à tout concept.
Le désordre réglé de ses branches n'obéit à aucun
Rythme. On passerait des siècles à figurer
Une raison à l'imagination qu'il proclame.
Sa liberté ne peut être qu'un absolu,
Enfermée qu'elle est dans des lois qui
Dépassent toute idée de loi.
        Pourquoi ces branches,
Ces bouquets, ce brouillard de feuilles, paroles du vent,
Cette broussaille de brindilles, balancée par l'hiver,
Qui avec la saison, reviendront plus touffues, plus hautes,
Et vertes, aussi longtemps que le bleu du ciel le permet?
Pour le savoir, faire un autre arbre,
Sur le même plan fou, dans toutes ses dimensions
Posant — toujours multipliée — la même énigme.
Puis d'autres, au lointain ou plus près,
Etagés de plein ou de vide selon
Les distributions dans l'espace,
Entre lesquels le regard s'insinuera comme les pas
D'une promenade. Où la lumière et les ombres
Portées par les choses s'allumeront et s'en iront
Tournant autour d'un axe. Où le monde
Sera tangible, sera chaud et froid,
Imprégné d'air invisible comme l'eau dans une éponge.
Qu'importe alors l'océan sans nom, le ciel
Sans doute inhabité, sinon d'astres problématiques,
Le pourquoi des prairies, de l'herbe dessinée
Au pied de l'arbre. Et l'arbre lui-même!
Que l'esprit s'ouvre aux évidences palpables,
Chaque curiosité autour de chaque chose enroulée,
Chaque désir satisfait d'être réalisable — peut-être —

The dark velvet surface is gradually peopled with millions —
If one but takes the trouble to view them in perspective —
Of distinct lives, mobile despite their roots,
Sparse in the shadows, without witnesses
But vibrant, spelling out with their sheen of watered silk
A tension beyond green and blue.

And the tree, born of the hand, tufted stain?
An accident?
                The tree eludes every concept.
The regulated disorder of its branches obeys no
Rhythm. One could spend centuries trying to deduce
A reason for the imagination it announces.
Its liberty can only be absolute,
Enclosed, as it is, in the laws which surpass
Every idea of law.
                Why these branches,
These bouquets, this fog of leaves, words of the wind,
This undergrowth of twigs swept away by winter,
That will return with the season, thicker, taller,
And green, as long as the blue of the sky allows it?
To know this, make another tree,
On the same mad scale in all its dimensions
Proposing the same enigma always multiplied.
Then others in the distance or closer,
Terraced in fullness or emptiness according to
Their distribution in space,
Among which the gaze insinuates itself as the steps
Of a stroll might. Where the light and the shadow
Cast by things will kindle and disappear turning around an axis
Where the world will be tangible and hot and cold,
Impregnated with invisible air like the water in a sponge.
What do they matter then, the nameless ocean and the sky,
Uninhabited, no doubt, except for problematic stars,
The why of the meadows, of the grass drawn
At the foot of the tree. And the tree itself!
You need only open your mind to the palpable
Evidence, each curiosity wrapped around each thing,
Each desire content to be realizable — perhaps —

Quelque part ailleurs que sous l'écrasant infini,
Toutes les fantaisies possibles, lacs, rochers,
Variété innombrable de verdures, changeant avec le temps,
Qu'il faudra dénombrer, qualifier avec autant
De nuances qu'elle en comporte, et peupler —
Alors que l'oeil dissipe la taie qui lui cache
Les hautes herbes sur les pentes près du fleuve,
Les algues au profond des eaux, les palmes et les fleurs —
De légions de serpents, d'escadrilles d'oiseaux.

Somewhere else than under crushing infinity
All the possible fantasies, lakes, cliffs,
Innumerable variety of verdure changing with the weather
Which will have to be counted, qualified with as many nuances
As they contain, and populated —
While the eye disperses the film that hides
The tall grasses on the slopes near the river,
The algae in the depths of the waters, the palms and the flowers —
With legions of serpents, with squadrons of birds.

DES NUITS ET DES CORPS

1

Le vent souffle sur mon écharpe ce soir
Comme la terre coule autour des oliviers
Une grande épée flamboie à contre-jour
Une pluie de lumière lavant les eucalyptus.

La voiture domine les falaises urbaines
Quand la nuit fait rentrer dans notre gorge le sang.
O ange qui déploie ses ailes hors de ses jeans
Tes mains sentent la truffe et le vin noir.

Les bouches cherchent leur profondeur secrète.
Le fumet des corps tendus bute sur la vitre
Les yeux se ferment sur une longue attente humide

Et notre vie chargée comme une caméra…

2

Je m'habillais pour une visite exemplaire
Et quittais, le corps parfumé, l'air de la chambre.
Le ciel noir, les cloches de tous les jours felées,
Pas un lampion ne restait allumé sur la place.

Comme un chat frôlant des papiers usés volant au vent
Le froid poudrait la rue de cristaux et de larmes.
La porte refermée la ville était à moi
L'espoir satinait l'eau vers l'absente Amérique.

Je portais, le long de rails qu'huilait la nuit,
Mon sang, fardeau vivant, et l'offrais à des lèvres
Tapies dans les buissons attendant le hasard
Pour s'ouvrir à cette vraie chaleur du monde.

OF NIGHTS AND BODIES

1

The wind blows on my scarf tonight
As earth flows around the olive trees
A big sword flashes against the light
A rain of light washing the eucalyptuses.

My car overlooks urban cliffs
When night puts the blood back in our throats.
O angel unfolding your wings out of your jeans
Your hands smell of truffles and black wine.

The mouths are searching their secret depth
The odor of stiffened bodies knocks against the car window
The eyes are closing on a long damp expectation

And our life is loaded like a camera...

2

I was getting dressed for an exemplary visit
And left, body perfumed, the air of the room.
Sky black, everyday bells sounding cracked,
Not a lantern still on in the square.

Like a cat rubbing against soiled papers lifted by the wind
The cold sprinkled the street with crystals and tears.
The door closed behind me the city was mine
Hope made the water satiny toward absent America.

I was carrying my blood along railways oiled by night
Like a living burden, and offered it to lips
Lurking in the bushes waiting for chance
To open themselves to that real warmth of the world.

3

Je raconte souvent à des inconnus dans la nuit
Une vie qui serait la mienne si j'étais un autre
Si j'avais pris d'autres chemins, si, par exemple,
J'avais refusé de garder dans ma main longuement

Le sang d'inconnus dans la nuit comme aujourd'hui.

Je déroule, baignant dans les lumières d'un faux passé
Paysages et visages, accidents et bonheurs,
Pour plaire à qui m'écoute et avec lui peut-être
Exorciser le temps.

        Or, toutes ces histoires
Ont l'unique parfum qui fait lever les mêmes
Rêves — éclairs oubliés, mémoires en délire,
Enfances lentes à nourrir autre que moi.

4

Dans combien de miroirs as-tu pris cette image
Mon ange, déguisé en complice? Qui t'a
Fourni l'explication de mes faiblesses?
Empruntes-tu mon sang pour mentir, ou prier?

Ma main, tu la voulais prompte à toutes caresses
Et mon corps tant mêlé à mon coeur dans nos lits
Que je ne sais plus qui de toi ou moi est moi
Innombrable animal que ma peur justifie.

Je te guette au sortir de sommeils sans témoin
Je te traîne dans les décharges de mes jours
Je te cloue aux cloisons dont demain m'environne
Je veux te garder vif en moi jusqu'à ma mort.

3

At night I often tell strangers the story
Of a life that would be mine if I were somebody else
If I had taken other roads, if, for example,
I had accepted to keep for long in my hand

The blood of unknown people in the night like today.

Bathing in the lights of a false past I unroll
Landscapes and faces, accidents and good fortune
To please the one who listens to me, and with him perhaps
To exorcise time.

Now, all these stories
Have the single perfume which is raising
The same dreams — forgotten lightning flashes, delirious memories,
Childhoods slow to nourish someone other than me.

4

In how many mirrors have you taken that picture
My angel disguised as an accomplice? Who has
Given you the explanation of my failings?
Are you borrowing my blood for a lie or a prayer?

You wanted my hand ready for every caress
And my body so mixed with my heart in our beds
That I don't know anymore who of you or me is I
Innumerable animal that my fear justifies.

I watch you coming out of sleeps without witnesses
I drag you in the dumping grounds of my days
I nail you to the partitions that tomorrow surrounds me with
I want to keep you alive in me until my death.

5

Découvre-moi comme un paysage par l'aube,
Retiens encore la nuit en ses ombres et laisse
Ton sang dans le matin révéler ses éclats.
Moi, j'atterris, — patience et passion butinées —
Dans l'éden ou l'enfer où je rêvais de toi,
Enrichissant de musc tes cheveux, et de lait
Ton corps, ma galaxie, mes lunes, mon soleil.

Le plaisir est un fleuve intemporel, ses rives
S'écroulent pour mêler les roches et les eaux.
Le coeur y perd son rythme et les mondes tournoient
Recréant le chaos initial où reposent
Nos têtes en explosion éternelle, mon tout…

6

Notre histoire a pu commencer dans l'hypothèse
D'un singe primordial aux rotules raidies
Contemplant par-delà les savanes brûlées
La derniére nuée qui blanchit l'horizon.
Il sent vibrer en son crâne un cristal où coule
La mesure du temps, la distance, son sang,
Le sable de ses jours et la désespérance
Les ossements ocrés testifiant qu'il vécut.

    "Que je me penche sur ta chaleur
    Toi, deuxième personne ouverte,
    Image à peine à moi semblable
    Toi seul à savoir que je meurs."

7

Recueillons-nous pour une immémoriale nuit,
Désirs tendus, brasiers jumeaux, commun silence.
Narguons nos corps. Qu'une épée de feu nous relie!

5

Uncover me as dawn uncovers a landscape,
Hold back once again the night in its shadows and let
Your blood in the morning reveal its shining.
I, I am landing — patience and passion plundered —
In the eden or hell where I was dreaming of you,
Enriching your hair with musk, and with milk
Your body, my galaxy, my moons, my suns.

Pleasure is a timeless river, its banks
Collapse to mix rock with waters.
There the heart loses its tempo and the worlds swirl
Recreating the initial chaos where our heads
Are resting in perpetual explosion, you my all…

6

Our story could have started in the hypothesis
Of a primordial ape with stiffened kneecaps
Gazing beyond the burnt savannas
At the last storm-cloud whitening on the horizon.
Who feels vibrating in its skull a crystal wherein flows
The measure of time, the distance, its blood,
The sands of its days and the despair
The ocher bones testifying that it was alive.

> "Let me lean on your warmth
> You, second open person,
> Image barely similar to myself
> You the only one to know that I am dying."

7

Let's gather ourselves for an immemorial night,
Desires outstretched, twin fire of live coals, shared silence.
Let's taunt our bodies. Let a sword of fire connect us!

La ville, en ses songes repue, ciel rougeoyant,
Construit ses jours futurs sur nos déjections.
Pas nous!
        Nous voulons habiter notre maison.
Un jardin y reçoit tous les oiseaux. La porte
En est transparente.
              Et le matin vient ranimer
Sur nos lèvres l'ardeur de nos corps à baiser.

Regards ouverts, accueillons le temps qui nous laisse
Le bonheur de nous être battus contre l'ombre
Sans verser une goutte de sang sur nos draps.

8

Il lacère en partant les odeurs du jardin
Comme un chat en chaleur marque son territoire.
Le citronnier flamboie d'un vert éteint, la menthe
Poivre à droite le bord du sentier jusqu'au thym.

La nuit a recélé d'insondables secrets
Le désir d'autres corps déborde tous les songes
Il regrette un fumet d'aisselles et de sang
Sa hantise depuis le tout premier matin.

      La lampe est tournée vers le mur
      Le drap relevé jusqu'au front
      Une photo montre des mains
      Un sexe lourd dans sa toison.

The city, in its dreams satiated, the sky reddening,
Is building on our dejecta its days to come.
Not us!
            We want to live in our house.
A garden is receiving every bird. The door
Is transparent.
                And morning comes to revive
On our lips the heat of our bodies for fucking.

With open eyes let's welcome the time that allows us
The luck of having fought against the darkness
Without spilling a drop of blood on our sheets.

8

Leaving he lacerates the scents of the garden
As a cat in heat marks its territory.
The lemon tree flashes a dull green light, the mint
Peppers the right edge of the path up to the thyme.

Night has hidden unfathomable secrets
The desire of other bodies overflows all the dreams
He misses a scent of armpits and of blood
His obsession since the very first morning.

        The lamp is turned toward the wall
        The sheet drawn up to the forehead
        A photograph shows hands
        A sex heavy in its mop.

COLLAGE

* A peindre cet éloignement
Qui auréole de non-être
Au plus profond des perspectives
Ce visage aussi flou qu'il est vu
Dans le souvenir
Puis s'estompant
Et c'est le temps
De dormir.

* Les maisons des marins au temps des catastrophes
Devaient ainsi de leurs fenêtres à secrets
Cligner pour regarder le soleil sur la mer.
Maintenant, les pupilles pillées de lumières,
Les rameurs mutinés nous lancent des injures...

* Le rideau se lève la scène représente
Un homme qui est un homme qui...
Et grâce à la vertu de miroirs parallèles
Un homme qui est un homme qui apostrophe
La distance de sa droite à sa gaucherie.

* Nul ne sait qui est près ou loin
Visage maison arbre ou homme
Nul ne sait qui est qui ou quoi
Ce sont les yeux qui toujours nous trahissent.

* Hors cadre de mon temps pour cet instant doré
Aucun musée n'aura le chef-d'œuvre achevé.
Pas un américain ne cachera dans ses caves
Un lendemain que n'aura signé aucun fou.

* Tout se conjugue au prétérit
Et rien ne commence
Rien qui n'est pas absolument
A la minute prècédant rien:
Le polygone dans ses lignes
Le cadavre entre les signes
Le brouillard dans mon désir.

COLLAGE

* To be painted: this remoteness
That haloes with non-being
In the deepest of perspectives
This face as blurred as it is seen
In memory
Then shading off
And it's time
To sleep.

* The sailors' houses in times of catastrophe
Should wink like that from their secret windows
To see the sun on the sea
Now, their pupils plundered of light,
The mutinous rowers heap insults on us...

* The curtain rises the scene represents
A man who is a man who...
And thanks to the virtue of parallel mirrors
A man who is a man who reprimands
The distance between his right and his left-handed clumsiness.

* Nobody knows who is near or far
Face house tree or man
Nobody knows who is who or what
It's always the eyes that betray us.

* Outside the frame of my time for that gilded instant
No museum will have the finished masterpiece.
No American will sequester in his cellar
A tomorrow that no fool will have signed.

* Everything is conjugated in the past tense
And nothing starts
Nothing which is not absolutely
In the minute preceding nothing:
The polygon in its lines
The corpse between the signs
The fog in my desire.

* Je tiens l'épaule appuyée
Sur l'épaule appuyée. Je tiens
Les sphères de mon monde extérieur
Trop verni pour qu'y plongent mes yeux…
Vers quoi va le soleil
Le vénérable Verbe
Berçant cet animal la crinière enthousiaste?

* Par un subterfuge de cause à effet
Et de cause des causes —
Suite gyroscopique ou spirale tournant
Aux notes d'une valse à façon d'alcool —
Devait naître et naquit la satiété hâtive
De boire et d'aimer et de penser normalement.
Mais argument rendu flou ou lassitude du coude
Il n'y eut de comparable à cette spontanée
Catastrophe un soir de bar
Que le processus d'auto-création
De Dieu.

* Un doigt sur les lèvres Adieu…
Puis cheminant à travers toits
La main sur les yeux et ta bouche
Adieu… jusqu'à la prochaine nuit.

Voleur brutal d'insomnie
L'escalier te hâle vers le dehors
Et la nuit te recueilles
Ainsi qu'un rusé pilleur d'espalier;

Les grands gendarmes étoilés
Te voient siffler des retraites à la Lune
Mais l'ombre de ma déchirure
Tombe en permanence sur le mur d'en face

Sera demain cruelle ouverte
Tellement que si tu entrais enfin
Dans le jardin des évidences
Tu en serais horrifié

Toi-même.

* I keep my shoulder leaning
Against the leaning shoulder. I keep
The spheres of my outer world
Too polished for my eyes to seize it...
Toward what is the sun moving,
The venerable Word
Cradling the animal with the enthusiastic mane?

* By a subterfuge from cause to effect
And from cause to causes —
Gyroscopic pursuit or spiral weaving
To the strains of a waltz in the alcoholic mode —
The premature surfeit of drinking and loving
And thinking normally would be and is born.
But, whether due to clouded arguments or weariness of elbow,
There was nothing comparable to that spontaneous
Catastrophe in a bar one evening
But the process of God's
Self-Creation.

* A finger at the lips Goodbye
Then wandering among roofs
Hand on my eyes and your mouth
Goodbye... until the next night

Brutal thief of insomnia
The stairway hauls you out
And night welcomes you as
An astute pillager of espaliers;

The big starry gendarmes
See you whistle retreat to the moon
But the shadow of my laceration
Falls forever on the opposite wall

Will be so cruelly open tomorrow
That if you finally entered
The garden of obvious facts
You'd be horrified

Yourself.

POEME

Comment dit-on en ce pays Demain?
Un prince sourd s'enchante au jeu des lèvres
L'argile roule aux hanches des potiers

Entrez ici il faut que la nuit tombe
Puisque sur une claie repose tel le jour
L'odeur le calme et la couleur des pommes

En ce pays comment dit-on Amour?
Ou chaque mot décuplant son pouvoir
Ecrase-t-il des idées qu'il exprime?

Ouvrez la voie aux saisons à l'instant
Que le silence à la chaleur emmèle
Chairs et cheveux mains membres et rubans

En soulevant cet amas de trophées
Vous déchirerez plus d'un monument
Et avec eux le clown méconnaissable

Debout devant le miroir joues ternies
Qui par dessus l'épaule avec candeur regarde
La cendre des diamants hier évanouis.

POEM

How do you say Tomorrow in this country?
A deaf prince is charmed by the play of lips
Clay is rolling at the potters' hips

Enter here night must fall since
The odor the stillness and the color of apples
Are resting on a wicker fruit-tray like the day

In this country how do you say Love?
Or does each word multiplying its power tenfold
Crush the ideas it expresses?

Open at once the way to the seasons
Let silence entangle
Flesh and hair hands limbs and ribbons with the heat

While lifting this pile of trophies
You'll rip up more than one monument
And with them the barely recognizable clown

Standing before the mirror cheeks dulled
Who looks with candor over his shoulder
At the ashes of the diamonds that vanished yesterday.

ENTR'ACTE

Son rêve avec le flamboyant
Le tapis rose éclaté
Lèvres paires

Il découvre le noir clavier
Les dents l'incendie éteint
Le miroir
Un tonnerre de théâtre.

Il est seul dans la salle.

Sa mère un lait lubrique
Un relent de vestale
Sur un versant
Anesthésié.

Il descend un volcan
Glaçon glissé dans sa culotte
Ardente quand paraît l'aube

Il danse une fable orientale.

Ses baisers
Il y boit palpitations
Et bave intarissable

Il souffle aussi le soir
Las trop longtemps trop lourd
De tout savoir neutre.

Il rit sous la pluie
Dans la plaine batave.

ENTR'ACTE

His dream with the flaming
The pink rug shattered
Even-numbered lips

He discovers the black keyboard
The teeth the extinguished conflagration
The mirror
Stage thunder.

He is alone in the hall.

His mother a libidinous milk
A musty smell of a vestal
On a slope
Anesthetized.

He climbs down a volcano
icecube slipped into his pants
Glowing when the sun rises

He's dancing an oriental fable.

His kisses
He drinks palpitations with them
And inexhaustible slobber.

He blows at evening also
Tired too long too heavy
With knowing everything's neutral.

He's laughing in the rain
In the Batavian plain.

NOCTURNE AMERICAIN

L'oiseau, son nom inconnu, couvre toute la nuit
De sa similitude avec un oiseau que je nomme
Dans ma mémoire ancestrale sans parvenir a évoquer
Ce parfum ancien que dispensait son chant. Cet oiseau-ci
Me semble un ami rencontré de frais avec lequel
Les paroles jamais ne remplaceront ce brillant
Des regards échangés en dépit de toute précaution.
Il m'inonde d'un musc végétal que je recueille
A chaque conjonction de branches et il paraît
Lui-même ressentir une jouissance fraternelle
A me savoir auprès de lui frémir dans son bonheur.

La nuit la rivière appelle l'homme ancien
Protégé par les dieux bénéfiques de la nuit.
Homme debout drapé dans l'immensité
Qu'il est seul à saisir, rivière, espace, nuit,
Et qu'il perçoit comme un aigle sa proie du haut
De toute son histoire d'homme à l'écoute
Des rivières, des monts, des sentiers qu'il a tracés,
De sa marque sur la terre qu'il est seul à connaître
Pas et pensées, pierres et rivières nommées,
Homme nommé, dieux créateurs à inventer
Pour prendre l'univers comme un poisson dans ses filets.

L'auto taille dans la forêt, dans la mer d'arbres traversée,
Le chemin où sont passées des tribus désorientées
Guidées par quelque Moïse vers la terre de miel et de lait
Que chante dans l'éther un cavalier aux cheveux de plumes.
Il me fait frémir comme les cordes d'une lyre,
Il me fait ouvrir les bras devant l'aurore qui s'annonce.
Au sortir de la forêt une pluie de cendres nous attend…
Retarde encore ce passage, et que j'entende
Un instant de plus le bruit de la rivière la nuit,
Au delà des arbres le pas des tribus. Que je sente
L'odeur musquée des hommes libres sur la terre…

AMERICAN NOCTURNE

The bird, its name unknown, covers the whole night
With its resemblance to a bird that I name
In my ancestral memory without managing to evoke
That ancient perfume its song dispenses. This bird
Seems to me a friend newly encountered with whom
Words will never replace the brightness
Of glances exchanged despite all precaution.
It floods me with a vegetal musk that I collect
At each forking of a branch and it seems
To experience a fraternal enjoyment of its own
Knowing I'm close to it trembling in its delight.

At night the river calls to the ancient man
Protected by the beneficent gods of the night.
Man standing draped in the immensity
That he alone grasps, river, space, night,
And that he perceives like an eagle its prey from the heights
Of his whole history of a man listening
To the rivers, mountains, paths he has traced,
Of his mark on the earth which he alone knows
Steps and thoughts, trees and rivers named,
Man named, creator gods to be invented
To seize the universe like a fish in his nets.

The car carves out of the forest, out of the traversed sea of trees,
The road where disoriented tribes have passed
Guided by some Moses toward the land of milk and honey
That a rider with hair of feathers sings of in the ether
He makes me tremble like the strings of a lyre
He makes me open my arms before the breaking dawn.
As we leave the forest a rain of ashes greets us...
Delays this passage further and may I hear
One moment more the sound of the river at night,
Beyond the trees the footfalls of tribes. May I smell
The musky odor of free men on earth...

ENTRE ELLE ET MOI

Elle approchait toutes les nuits
Les pieds bandés la bouche peinte
Pour doucement souffler sur mes sourcils
Et m'éveiller sans m'effrayer

Douce amère vertu
Au ventre lisse ceint
D'une cordelette magique
Qu'il ne fallait surtout pas dénouer

Et pendant l'étreinte mes mains
Mes dents mon sexe se mouraient
De ne pouvoir résoudre ce mystère
Ni même de comprendre qu'il y en avait un

Elle s'éloignait avant le matin
Le dos lacéré les flancs ensanglantés
A pas tranquille sans sourire
Et me laissait avec les gouttes

D'un onguent tombé de sa ceinture
Au bord du lit souillé où je pouvais entendre
Le jour lourd de questions se lever.

BETWEEN HER AND ME

Each night she drew near
Bandaged feet painted mouth
To blow gently on my eyebrows
And wake me without frightening me

Bittersweet virtue
With smooth waist encircled
With a magic cord that above all
Must not be untied

And during the embrace my hands
My teeth my sex were dying
Of not being able to solve this mystery
Or even know if there was one

She left before morning
Her back lacerated her sides bleeding
On calm steps without smiling
And left me with the drops

Of an ointment fallen from her sash
On the edge of the soiled bed where I could hear
The sun rising, heavy with questions.

RECITATIF ET AIR DES LARMES

I *Récitatif*

Les flammes se sont glissées
Dans nos chambres à coucher
Comme serpents chassés des buissons du Sinai.
Elles ont fait de nos corps un subtil amalgame
De molécules rendues à l'univers originel,
Et, notre esprit ayant rejoint le choeur des anges,
Avons-nous ri et pleuré devant la terre caramélisée,
Pomme trop cuite le four était trop chaud,
Etoile réduite en cendres, à un trou noir!

Pourtant c'était un paysage
Si confortable à habiter!
De puantes fumées enténébraient les soleils,
Les lignes de crête urbaine portaient des clochers
Où le vent faisait tinter des hymnes contradictoires.
Le soir ouvert laissait passer en files
Le troupeau de fourmis vers le miel des écrans…
Il y avait aussi derrière des monts préservés
La trace de skis montrant le chemin vers le lac
Noir où les constellations se dédoublaient
Et le bord de la mer où nous marchions casque aux oreilles
— You remember? — pour nous protéger du fracas
Répercuté entre les pics statistiques:
Cris, pleurs arrachés aux entrailles de nos terreurs.

J'habitais un palais ancien aux moucharabiehs bleus.
Les fenêtres donnaient face aux îles sur la plage.
De mon lit je voyais les garçons nus briser la vague
Et les filles sous des parasols boire à des pailles.
J'attendais une femme en un jardin. C'était le jour.
Un oiseau s'installait dans le feuillage.
J'appelais sans le savoir des instants de bonheur.
Puis un matin le soleil disparu ne revint pas.
Nuit incompréhensible. La main cherchant d'autres mains
Ne rencontrait dans les rues que membres disloqués
Un mur brûlant sur lequel nos ongles lacéraient
Nous ne savions plus quelle image. Seul

RECITATIVE AND ARIA OF THE TEARS

I *Recitative*

The flames slipped
Into our bedrooms
Like serpents chased from the bushes of Sinai
They turned our bodies into a subtle alloy
Of molecules returned to the original universe,
And, once our minds had rejoined the angelic choir,
We laughed and wept before the caramelized earth
An apple baked too long in a too-hot oven,
Star reduced to ashes, to a black hole!

Nevertheless it was such a comfortable
Landscape to live in!
Stinking fumes darkened the suns,
The urban skylines carried steeples
Where the wind made contradictory hymns ring out.
The open evening let the flocks of ants
Pass through in single file toward the honey of TV screens...
There were also behind the preserved mountains
The tracks of skis showing the way to the black
Lake where the constellations unfolded
And the edge of the sea where we walked wearing headsets
You remember? — to protect us from the din
Reverberating among the peaks of statistics:
Cries, sobs torn from the entrails of our terrors.

I lived in an ancient palace with blue moucharabiehs.
The windows looked out over the beach to the islands.
From my bed I saw naked boys fend the waves
And girls under parasols drinking through straws.
I was waiting for a woman in a garden. It was the day.
A bird settled in the foliage.
Without knowing it I called these moments of happiness.
Then one morning the vanished sun didn't come back.
Incomprehensible night. A hand groping for other hands
Found only dislocated limbs in the streets
A burning wall on which our nails scratched
An image we no longer recognized. Only

Un vrombissement à vomir, une boule de feu obscur
Roulait sur les pavés et le visage des hommes.

II *Air des Larmes*

Putain aux faux cils perdus
Dans le désordre de nos lits
Qui promettait des plaisirs
Des richessese et des honneurs
Tu nous disait t'appeler Vie
Et les aveugles les sourds t'avaient crue
T'avaient suivie sans y penser
Il ne nous reste qu'à pleurer
Si nous avions encore des yeux
Dans le désordre de nos lits.

Comment effacer ce désastre?
Comment revenir au berceau
Au calme des premières eaux
A la création des astres?
Et repartir pour un autre destin
Comment rêver au lendemain
A l'autre ciel à l'autre plage
A la chaleur d'un vrai soleil
Comment fuir la ville qui brûle?
Comment revenir au berceau?

A sickening hum, a ball of dark fire
Rolled along the paving-stones and on the faces of men.

II *Aria of the tears*

Whore with false eyelashes lost
In the disorder of our beds
Who promised pleasures
Riches and honors
You told us to call you Life
And the blind and the deaf had believed you
Had followed you without thinking
We have nothing left to do but cry
If we still had eyes
In the disorder of our beds.

How to erase this disaster?
How to return to the cradle
To the calm of the first waters
To the creation of the stars?
And leave again for another destiny
How to dream of tomorrow
Of the other sky the other beach
Of the heat of a true sun
How to flee the burning city?
How to return to the cradle?